Opening the Door to Bön

Opening the Door to Bön

Latri Khenpo

Geshe Nyima Dakpa Rinpoche

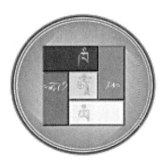

Snow Lion Publications
Ithaca, New York
Boulder, Colorado

Snow Lion Publications
P.O. Box 6483
Ithaca, NY 14851 USA
(607) 273-8519
www.snowlionpub.com

Printed in U.S.A. on acid-free recycled paper.

ISBN-10 1-55939-246-0
ISBN-13 978-1-55939-246-4

Library of Congress Cataloging-in-Publication Data

Dakpa, Nyima, 1962-
    Opening the door to Bön / Nyima Dakpa.
       p. cm.
    ISBN-13: 978-1-55939-246-4 (alk. paper)
    ISBN-10: 1-55939-246-0 (alk. paper)
    1. Spiritual life—Bon (Tibetan religion) I. Title.
BQ7982.2.D35 2006
299.5'4—dc22   2005026683

Contents

Foreword

By His Holiness the 33rd Menri Trizen, Abbot of Menri

In this book, Latri Khenpo Geshe Nyima Dakpa Rinpoche has detailed both the outer and inner fundamental practices of Bön. These are methods to achieve enlightenment and detach oneself from the suffering of cyclic existence, by means of following the teacher as a source of wisdom and realizing further gains through practice.

In short, all deeds should be based on virtue and the true pathway should be followed with pure intention. One begins with the Fourfold Practices of the outer preliminary practices in order to tame one's ordinary thoughts.

Subsequently, one practices the generation of the mind of enlightenment, which is the entry to the pathway of the greater vehicles, and the practice of Lamai Naljor, through which one can achieve self-realization, and all of the other inner foundational practices that follow.

This book will be of great benefit to practitioners, both for themselves and for helping others as well.

With appreciation and blessings,

33rd Menri Trizen Lungtok Tenpai Nyima Rinpoche
Spiritual Head of Bön

Acknowledgments

In the winter of 2000 I traveled to Los Angeles to have surgery, after which I recovered and rested at the home of my student David Peteler. During that time, David encouraged me to start this book — a book that I had long planned to write — to provide an introduction and doorway to the view and practice of Bön. His willingness to help with the project encouraged me to begin the first draft. He very kindly worked long hours to type my notes and edit the first draft of the text. I would like to thank him for his time and effort. I also give thanks to his wife Deborah for her patience, her care for my health, and for facilitating my stay.

I want to thank my long-time host, Barbara Bradshaw, for always being very supportive of my traveling to teach and work in the United States. She has taken care of me in so many ways. I also thank her specifically for further editing my book during my stay in her home, contributing many useful suggestions and corrections.

The main work in editing this book was done by my long-time friend Sue Anna Harwood. She spent many hours editing and providing suggestions and clarifications. I appreciate her support from the core of my heart. Unfortunately, Sue Anna passed away before she could see this work published.

I thank Anita Guzmann for working diligently for hours from the very beginning to edit and format the manuscript. She has worked enthusiastically on every level to achieve its completion.

I thank my host and supporter Elisabeth Adelsberger, who encouraged and supported me and facilitated all my needs during my stay in her home in Vienna, Austria. I also thank her son Stephan, who spent a lot of time on his computer helping me.

I wish to thank Nyima Wöser Chökhortshang for data input and editorial assistance.

I wish to thank Mr. and Mrs. Huang for generously providing their home and complete hospitality to me in Great Neck, NY, which enabled me to complete the final editing.

I wish to thank David Kozowski for his tireless effort with the final editing and all his editorial assistance.

Last but not least, I want to thank Geshe Denma Gyaltsen La, the Abbot of Zhu Ri Sheng Yungdrung Kundak Ling Bön Monastery in Sikkim, India, who has accompanied and assisted me for several years during my travels for teaching and work. He has always given me genuine support and encouragement. He has worked with me and all the others involved with this book to move the project forward, always helping on every level as needed. I am very grateful for his true love and kindness. This book would not exist without his diligent effort and support.

There are many other people who helped significantly but whose names are not mentioned here. I thank them all. Without the tireless help and support of many people, this book would not have been written and published.

It is my utmost hope that whoever reads this book will gain some benefit from it in their practice.

Mu Tsuk Mar Ro (May all beings be happy).

Latri Khenpo Geshe Nyima Dakpa

About the Author

In the Tibetan tradition, the students' knowledge of the lineage and personal history of a teacher is important, in part because it instills confidence with regard to the authenticity and qualifications of the teacher. While this subject is addressed more fully hereafter, the following autobiography may prove useful in this regard. — Editors

My name is Latri Khenpo Nyima Dakpa Rinpoche. I am the Abbot and lineage holder of Latri Monastery in the Derge area of the Kham region of Eastern Tibet.

I grew up in the first Bön refugee community in Nepal, located in Dorpatan. My family is the lineage holder of the Latri lineage. My father, Latri Gyaltsen Nyima, was the third reincarnation of Tsultrim Phuntsok, a great practitioner of Eastern Tibet. When I was six years old, I began learning to read and write Tibetan. At this time I also started my religious studies under the guidance of my father and Tsultrim Nyima Rinpoche, the Abbot of the monastery at Dorpatan. When I was thirteen, I moved with my family to Kathmandu, Nepal, where I worked in a sweater business and also mastered the art of carpet design.

The Bönpos (followers of Bön) now living in Kathmandu originally lived in the Dorpatan area. Most of them are devotees of Tewa Monastery, located in the upper region of Tibet. My father held the position of a lama of Tewa Monastery. Since there were no other Bön monasteries in Kathmandu at that time, he assumed the responsibilities for all the annual Bön religious activities. His goal was to keep the Bönpo community close together and for the young people in the community to have a firm connection to their original Bön culture. For that reason he and three elders established the Bönpo community Te Bön Kyi Dug and took care of all spiritual ceremonies for the people of Tewa until he died in 1987. This organization is still active today in Kathmandu. It participates in all religious activities at Triten Norbutse Monastery and serves Bönpos in as many ways as it can.

When I was fifteen, my father took me to Menri Monastery in Dolanji, Himachal Pradesh, India, to be ordained as a monk and educated there. As my father was getting older and did not know what was going to happen to Tibet in the future, he wanted me to become a spiritual master and skilled religious practitioner so that I could be of service to the Bönpo community. However, I became very homesick and eventually returned home to Kathmandu.

In 1977 the senior Menri Lopon, H.E. Sangye Tenzin Rinpoche, sent a message to my father asking him why I had not become a monk yet. My father then expressed that it was his wish that I return to the monastery to become a fully ordained monk. I was very touched by this, and I realized that as the eldest son with the name of the lineage holder Latri, it was my duty to become a monk and serve the Bönpos. I knew within my heart that it was the proper time for me to accept this responsibility. That same evening, at a family gathering, my father talked about the message from Ponlop Sangye Tenzin Rinpoche and added that it had always been his wish that I become a monk. He said, "If you were to take monks' vows, it would make me happier than if I had been given the size of a sheep's head in gold." My entire family encouraged me to accept the challenge, and I decided to return to Menri Monastery in Dolanji.

In September 1977 I arrived at Menri Monastery and went to visit His Holiness the 33rd Menri Trizin, Sangye Tenzin Rinpoche, the spiritual head of the Bön tradition. H.E. Yongzin Tenzin Namdak Rinpoche, the head teacher of the monastery, and H.E. Sangye Tenzin Rinpoche welcomed me and blessed me with the traditional white scarves. My aunt and I visited with Sangye Tenzin Rinpoche and asked for a prayer of blessings to allow me to be successful in my wish to become a monk. In response, H.E. Sangye Tenzin Rinpoche promised to give me a precious gift, and he poured a whole vase of blessed water over my head.

During the observance of Tibetan New Year, on the birthday of the Second Lord, Nyamed Sherab Gyaltsen, which is the fifth day of the first month of the Tibetan calendar, I took the vows to become a monk from H.H. the 33rd Menri Trizin and H.E. Yongzin Tenzin Namdak Rinpoche. Since that day, I have been cared for and guided by H.H. the 33rd Menri Trizin, the spiritual head of Bön.

In 1978 I was among the first students to enter the newly founded Bön Dialectic School, the monastery school where philosophy

(Dho, Ngag, and Dzogchen), astrology, medicine, and all the other traditional Bön disciplines are taught. There I received all my teachings from H.E. Yongzin Tenzin Namdak Rinpoche and Lharam Geshe Yungdrung Nam Gyal.

I made a commitment not to take any vacation before graduating from the Bön Dialectic School. Even when my parents wrote to ask me to join the family for the Tibetan New Year festivities, I kept this promise and did not join them. I did not return home until 1987 after having received my Geshe degree, which is the equivalent of a Ph.D. degree.

Since 1978 I have been assisting H.H. the 33rd Menri Trizin with the administration of the Monastic Centre as well as Central School for Tibetans (CST) in Dolanji. I also represent His Holiness at meetings and conferences held away from Dolanji. Furthermore, I was of service to the orphanage until my graduation from the monastery.

In 1982 my father and brother Lhakpa traveled to Tibet to visit Latri Monastery and the people still living there. I had received several letters from these people, asking me to join them in Tibet to take over the responsibility of educating the young monks of the monastery. For this reason I traveled to Tibet in 1987. There, in addition to visiting Latri Monastery, I also made a tour of thirty-eight other monasteries. The purpose of these visits was to strengthen the communication and connection between the Bön monasteries in India and those in Tibet. My most important visits were to Menri Monastery as well as Latri Monastery, where I was enthroned as Abbot.

In 1988 I returned to Menri Monastery in Dolanji. In April of the same year His Holiness the Dalai Lama visited the monastery. During this visit, H.H. the 33rd Menri Trizin discussed the school system of Dolanji with H.H. the Dalai Lama. The school had only six grades and H.H. the 33rd Menri Trizin asked for permission to add grades 7 and 8, so that the children would have even more opportunity to study their original Bön culture. H.H. the Dalai Lama agreed to the project and wished that as many children as possible could be brought to Dolanji to be raised according to the Bön culture. The Education Minister of the Tibetan Government-in-Exile at that time, Juchen Thupten, gave ten thousand rupees for the project. H.H. the Dalai Lama added that this money was given to mark the beginning of a new project.

At the request of the people of Dolanji, H.H. the 33rd Menri Trizin entrusted me with the official permit to expand the school. All the necessary documents were filed with the Indian government, and I was assigned the responsibility to gather children from the different Bönpo communities to be sent to attend the Bön school in Dolanji. I made an official visit to Kathmandu in order to talk to the local Bönpo community about the project and spread this information to Bönpo communities in Dolpo, Lubrak, Zomsom, and Tankye, as well as remote areas of Nepal, Bhutan, Sikkim, and India.

In addition to the school project, H.H. the 33rd Menri Trizin gave me the assignment to set up a home for girls and boys in Dolanji so that they would have the opportunity to receive an education. This was in perfect harmony with my own desire to help and sustain Bön children, and I was more than pleased to accept the task. In 1988 I established the home known today as the Bön Children's Home. This is the first and only Bön organization that raises both boys and girls together. Here they not only find a place to receive an education, but also a real home. I still serve as Director of the Bön Children's Home.

Most of the children at the Bön Children's Home are from very remote Bönpo communities such as Dolpo and Lubrak in Nepal. In the beginning, there were forty-five children. Today the number has grown to 253 children between five and twenty years of age. Some of them have already been graduated from the school in Dolanji and are continuing their education in Shimla, Varanasi, and Dehradun. I also serve as the chairman of the local advisory committee of the Central School for Tibetans in Dolanji.

In 1987 I created and became the editor of "Bön Go" ("Door to Bön"), the only Bön magazine published in the Tibetan language. The publication team currently has six members and will soon publish the sixteenth issue of the magazine.

In May 1996 I was assigned by H.H. the 33rd Menri Trizin to establish the Mongyal Monastery in Dehradun, India, on land that was donated for the project by the Prince of Lingtsang and the Tibetan Kham Lingtsang Society in 1974. The project aims to reestablish the original and unique educational system of Mongyal Monastery in Tibet.

In 2002, with the blessings of H.H. the 33rd Menri Trizin, I oversaw the construction of a new three-story school building and playground in Dolanji, which included adding a fence around the school's campus. Also, after much administrative consultation, we were able to expand our CST from the elementary and middle-school grades to include secondary grades nine and ten. We hope to expand further by adding grades eleven and twelve, and thus have a complete high school.

Since 1991 I have traveled yearly to the United States and various countries in Europe, such as Austria, France, Germany, Poland, Belarus, Moscow, Ukraine, and Switzerland, in order to spread the teaching of Bön and raise funds for the Bön Children's Home. I return regularly to give teachings at the Bön centers that I have founded. These are the Yeru Bön Center in Los Angeles (U.S.), Shen Chen Ling in Minsk (Belarus), Bön Shen Ling in Moscow (Russia), and the Shen Ten Ling Bön Centre in Vienna (Austria).

Readers who wish to contact Latri Khenpo Geshe Nyima Dakpa Rinpoche may do so through the following Bön centers:

In the United States:
Yeru Bön Center
1866 N. Ave 56
Los Angeles, CA 90042-1121
(323) 255-3553

In Europe:
Shen Tenling Bön Center in Vienna
Herbeckstrasse 60
A-1100 Wien, Austria
+43 (01) 4786260

In India:
    Bön Children's Home
    Dolanji, P.O. Kotla Panjola
    Via Oachghat Solan
    H.P. 173223, India
    +91-1799 253056

Introduction

This book is dedicated to those who are interested in learning about the Bön religion. It may be of value both to beginning practitioners and to those interested in acquiring a general knowledge of Bön.

According to our tradition, the Bön religion has existed in this world for 18,000 years. Yungdrung Bön originated as the teachings of Tönpa Shenrab in Olmo Lung Ring. From there the teachings spread to Zhang Zhung and from there throughout most Asian lands.

For generations, all Tibetans were believers and practitioners of Bön. There are two main ways to practice Bön: one takes monastic vows and lives and practices in a monastery, or one lives as a layperson with one's family.

Bön has nine different levels, also known as the nine ways of Bön. These levels enable one to practice gradually, according to one's capacity for understanding. The essence and purpose of the Bön teachings is to introduce the practitioner to the reality of existence and the nature of mind through a process of overcoming the five poisons. The world is realized to be like a mirror in which is seen one's own face through reflection. One learns to point one's finger always at oneself rather than others.

One takes gradual steps when starting to learn and practice Bön. Further practice and realization provide the basis for solid understanding. In the beginning, all practitioners receive teachings on the preliminary practices (Ngöndro). Then meditation practices are added that focus on the true nature of mind. It is necessary to have a qualified teacher when beginning these practices, in order to receive an introduction to the nature of mind. Through practice, one begins to gain self-realization of the natural state of mind and eventually overcomes the unhappiness, depression, and pressures that individuals suffer in this cyclic existence.

The final stage is the practice of Phowa, known as the rainbow transformation. This is a method to transform one's mind consciousness into the true essence of enlightenment. It is an important practice in our day-to-day life, as it provides us with experience that benefits our minds.

Since 1990, I have traveled to the United States and other western countries, giving teachings and lectures at many universities, spiritual centers, private homes, and other venues. During that time, I have met many people who are interested in studying and following the traditions of both Buddhism and Bön. I see in many a lack of basic knowledge about the foundation of the practice, such as the importance of trust and faith, realization of the four practices, understanding the rareness of the opportunity of the perfect human condition for perfecting one's mind, and so on.

I realized that it would be very helpful to have a guidebook that explains how to practice effectively according to the Bön teachings and emphasizes the methods of our basic practices and their importance. Without a stable foundation and an understanding of the practice, one's understanding of these teachings will not develop further. This is similar to constructing a building: without a strong foundation, one will not be able to build many stories and the structure will not be stable and lasting. This also applies to one's spiritual practice.

In this book, I mainly focus on the importance of a genuine and correct attitude while receiving the teachings and during practice, and offer a detailed explanation of the rare opportunity of having a perfect human body. Additionally, I discuss the foundation practices to purify impure thoughts on the basis of compassion and love and then generate the mind of enlightenment.

I have tried to use the native language of Tibet along with the English translations throughout the book, especially for terms describing practices or aspects of mind, in order to familiarize readers with the original language used to describe the ideas and practices discussed here. However, many Tibetan terms do not have a direct translation into English. Tibetan words are spelled phonetically, not as scholars would romanize them. It is hoped that this will make it easier for readers unfamiliar with the Tibetan language to pronounce and remember the important terms.

My hope is that this book will be useful for those who wish to enter into the vastness of Bön. May all readers learn and use the wisdom teachings presented here for the benefit of themselves and all sentient beings.

Chapter 1

Origin and History of Bön

OLMO LUNG RING

Yungdrung Bön, the root culture and religion of Tibet, originated from the teachings of Tönpa Shenrab, who was born in a completely pure and spiritual land named Tagzig Olmo Lung Ring (hereafter Olmo Lung Ring), which is beyond the impure nature of this existing world. The birthplace of all the enlightened ones, it is a perfected realm where peace and true joy last forever, and it is free from any danger of destruction by any of the elements of nature.

The land of Olmo Lung Ring lies to the west of Mount Kailash and is in the shape of an eight-petaled lotus divided into four parts: the inner, middle, and outer parts, and the boundary. Its sky is like an eight-spoked wheel. Olmo Lung Ring is filled with beautiful gardens, stupas, parks, and snow-covered mountains. Yungdrung Gutsek, a pyramid-shaped mountain with nine Yungdrungs ascending like a staircase to the top, is in the center of Olmo Lung Ring. While a single Yungdrung symbolizes the everlasting and indestructible essence of mind, the nine Yungdrungs symbolize the nine ways or stages of Bön. On each step of the mountain are temples of both male and female deities, and beautiful stupas that symbolize the mind of enlightenment.

Four rivers flow from Yungdrung Gutsek. The mountain has four sides that face in the four directions, and these rivers flow from the corners at the mountain's base, from formations that resemble the heads of four different animals. From the east, the snow lion is the source of the river Narazara; from the north, the horse is the source of the river Pakshi; from west, the peacock is the source of the river Gyim Shang; and from the south, the elephant is the source of the river Sindhu.

Some scholars identify Mount Kailash in northwestern Tibet as Olmo Lung Ring, due to the lakes and snow-covered mountains that surround the area and the four rivers that flow from it. The followers of Bön do not accept this explanation. This is because Olmo Lung Ring is not a physical place that can be visited by ordinary human beings. In order to reach Olmo Lung Ring, one must practice, become purified of all negativities, and achieve enlightenment. Bönpos pray to be born in Olmo Lung Ring because this can occur only after achieving enlightenment. Visiting Mount Kailash is possible before enlightenment is reached, as long as one is determined to accept the physical challenges. This is proof to Bönpos that Mount Kailash is not Olmo Lung Ring.

Historical Bön texts state very clearly that the holy mountain Mount Kailash was in the center of the kingdom of Zhang Zhung, which was the closest neighboring kingdom to Tibet and existed until the end of the eighth century. Zhang Zhung was integrated into Tibet after the death of Emperor Ligmincha, its last ruler. In early times, the kingdom of Zhang Zhung extended from what is today the upper part of western Tibet through parts of Nepal, northern India (Kashmir, Ladakh, Zanskar, Kinnaur, Spiti, etc.), to Pakistan (Kashmir) and to China (the Karakoram area). Most of the Bön teachings have been translated from the Zhang Zhung language into Tibetan.

Mount Kailash is a holy place for Bönpos and is blessed by the Zhang Zhung deity Me Ri. The Me Ri teachings were among the main practices of the Zhang Zhungpa (people of Zhang Zhung) and were later were introduced into Tibet. The lineage of this practice has been preserved, and it continues to the present time.

TÖNPA SHENRAB MIWO CHE, FOUNDER OF THE BÖN RELIGION

Long ago in a part of heaven called Sidpa Yesang, there were three brothers named Dakpa, Salwa, and Shepa. Their father was Sidpa Triöd and their mother was Kunshe. These brothers studied under a great teacher named Tobumtri Log Gi Che Chen. After completing their studies, they went to Shen Lha Ökar, the Enlightened One of Compassion, and asked how they could be of the greatest assistance in liberating sentient beings from the suffering of the cyclic world. He advised them to take human birth in three different ages so that each brother could help the sentient beings of that age achieve liberation. Following Shen Lha Ökar's advice,

7

Dakpa, the elder brother, was born as a teacher of the past age, and took the name Tönpa Togyal Ye Khyen. The second son, Salwa, was born in this present age as Tönpa Shenrab. Shepa will be born in a future age as Thangma Medon.

Salwa manifested as a blue cuckoo and along with his two disciples, Malo and Yulo, went to the top of Mount Meru, where he deliberated as to where and to what parents he should be born. Through his wisdom, he foresaw that he would be born in the heart of Olmo Lung Ring in a palace called Barpo Sogyed, located on the south side of Mount Yungdrung Gutsek. His father would be Gyalbon Thökar, and his mother, Yochi Gyalzhed Ma.

Two texts, *Dho Zermig* and *Dho Due*, contain biographies of Tönpa Shenrab, who was born in Olmo Lung Ring at dawn on the day of the full moon in the first month of the Tibetan calendar. This was the year of the male wood mouse. More than 18,000 years have passed since that time. He married at a young age and had eight sons, who became his most important successors and spread his teachings, and two daughters. At the age of thirty-one, he renounced the cyclic world and became a monk. He cut his hair himself and took off his princely robes, offering them in the ten directions for the benefit of all sentient beings. He then distributed all his princely belongings to people in need.

The Enlightened Ones of the Ten Directions (Chok Chu Dewar Shekpa) were pleased with his offering and in appreciation of this and other great deeds (such as detaching himself from the material world), they blessed him. The six robes (naza gö drug) and the five objects (rinchen ze nga) of a monk descended to him from the sky. This initiated the Bön rules regarding monks' robes and material possessions. Since then, the tradition of these rules has been preserved without interruption.

Tönpa Shenrab made one trip to Tibet during his lifetime. A demon called Khyap Pa Lag Ring stole Tönpa Shenrab's horses and took them to the Kongpo Valley in Tibet. Tönpa Shenrab shot an arrow to make a path through the mountains. This is referred to as the "pathway of the arrow of light" or Öser Da Lam. When Tönpa Shenrab visited the Kongpo Valley, he pacified the demons and evil spirits that inhabited Tibet. He blessed a mountain in the Kongpo Valley now known as the "Bön Mountain of Kongpo" or Kongpo Bön Ri. Bönpos and Buddhists still make pilgrimages to Kongpo Bön Ri, circumambulating the mountain counterclockwise in the Bön manner. Self-appearing recitation prayers and images of deities can be seen on the rocks, from which pilgrims can receive blessings. In the center of the mountain is a special rock known as "The Heart of Kuntu Zangpo." One can see three essential recitations and a statue of the Enlightened One of the Six Realms on this rock. There are also five caves, blessed by Tönpa Shenrab, where people still practice. One cave is found at each of the four directions, while the last is in the center of these four. By practicing even one or two hours here, one can achieve more blessings than in any other place.

During his only visit to Tibet, Tönpa Shenrab gave blessings and teachings: purifying the environment, making smoke offerings to local spirits, erecting prayer flags, exorcising evil spirits, etc. He stopped the local tradition of offering animal sacrifices, and taught the offering of ransom and red torma instead. This satisfied the evil spirits, who had been causing illness and misfortune.

Tönpa Shenrab brought many kinds of ceremonies, ritual

performances, and religious dances that spread rapidly throughout Tibet. No form of Buddhism outside Tibet shares these traditions. The only reasonable explanation for this is that these ceremonies became rooted and preserved in the Bön culture after Tönpa Shenrab's visit. Tibetan Bönpos have practiced these rites from generation to generation, and do so even to this day.

Determining that the Tibetans were not yet ready to receive the full teachings of Bön, Tönpa Shenrab prophesied that in the future his teachings would flourish in Tibet. Then he returned to Olmo Lung Ring. In order to demonstrate impermanence, Tönpa Shenrab passed away at the age of eighty-two. Measured in Olmo Lung Ring time, eighty-two years equates to 8,200 human years.

Tönpa Shenrab performed many great deeds in his whole life, but among the most well known are "The Twelve Great Deeds" (Zedpa Chunyi). More details about theses deeds are given in the three sources of his biography: the short one (*Dho Dhe* or The Epitome of Aphorism), rediscovered in the tenth century, in one volume; the medium one (*Dho Zermig* or The Piercing Eye), rediscovered in the eleventh century, in two volumes; and the long one (*Zi Jid* or Glorious), given through oral transmission by Tulku Lodhen Nyingpo in the fourteenth century, in twelve volumes.

Bön Teachings and Their History

Tönpa Shenrab turned the wheel of Bön in three gradual periods: firstly, up to age twelve, he specifically gave teachings on relative truth (kunzob denpa); secondly, from age thirteen to thirty-one, he mainly gave teachings on absolute truth (dondam denpa); thirdly, from age thirty-two to eighty-two, he gave teachings on the ultimate state of liberation (dol lam). Thus, Tönpa Shenrab turned the final wheel of Bön by teaching jointly on both relative and absolute truth.

The Bön teachings are often categorized as four doors, with the fifth door as the treasure (Go Zhi Zöd Dang Nga). However, all the Bön teachings are inclusively taught in nine gradual stages, known as the nine ways of Bön (Bön Tekpa Rim Gu). These are further divided into four causal ways and five result or fruition ways as follows.

- Cha Shen Tekpa,
- Nang Shen Tekpa,
- Trul Shen Tekpa, and
- Sid Shen Tekpa

are known as the causal ways (Gyui Tekpa Zhi). These practices engender inspiration and trust. One becomes well grounded in one's daily life through these practices.

- Ghenyen Tekpa,
- Drangsong Tekpa,
- Ahkar Tekpa,
- Yeshen Tekpa, and
- Dzogchen Yang Tsei Lamed Kyi Tekpa

are known as the ways of fruition or result (Drewu Tekpa Nga). These are higher-level teachings based on the faith and trust developed through the first four ways. The ninth is the highest and most secret, esoteric way of fruition.

These nine ways contain all levels of teachings from the simplest to the highest view, and are well known in all regions of Tibet.

Examples of Bön practices include putting up prayer flags, making purification smoke offerings to the protectors and deities, making medicine, and performing divinations and astrological readings. Also included are many ritual ceremonies such as those for healing, long life, weddings, and harmonizing the environment and the universe. Esoteric practices include death-ritual ceremonies to liberate dead persons from suffering as well as exorcism, consecration, and empowerment. But Bön practices are not limited to ceremonies and rituals only. There are higher-level teachings of a very esoteric nature, in both Tantra (Sang Ngag) and the Great Perfection (Dzogchen). Sang Ngag includes visualization and generation (kyerim) and perfection (zogrim) stages and the practices of channels (tsa), wind (lung), and physical exercise (trulkhor) as gradual practices on the wheels or chakras (khorlo), energy points in the body. The most secret Bön practice is Dzogchen, the great perfection. All of these traditions are still preserved and practiced today.

Eighteen-hundred years after the passing of Tönpa Shenrab, Mucho Demdug came from heaven to Olmo Lung Ring as the speech emanation of Tönpa Shenrab. Mucho Demdug turned the wheel of Bön so that all the teachings of Tönpa Shenrab would be organized and classified. He taught many students, the best known of which are referred to as the Six Great Scholars or the "Six Ornaments of the World" (Zamling Khepi Gyendug). They translated the Bön teachings into their own languages and spread them throughout their native lands. These six great masters are Mutsa Tahe, Tritok Partsa, and Huli Paryag from Tagzig; Lhadag Ngagdo from India; Legtang Mangpo from China; and Sertok Chejam from Trom.

The Bön teachings were by now well established in Zhang Zhung, where the northwestern part of modern Tibet is today. As noted above, Zhang Zhung was an independent state with its own language, literature, and culture. It was divided into three sections, referred to as the "three doors": inner (phugpa), outer (gopa), and middle (barpa). The inner door is Olmo Lung Ring, the middle door is Tagzig, and the outer door is Zhang Zhung itself. In the eighth century, the assassination of Emperor Ligmincha by the Tibetan king Trisong Dewutsen ended Zhang Zhung's independence. Thereafter, Zhang Zhung's land and culture were assimilated into Tibet, and they eventually disappeared. However, many Zhang Zhung words from ancient Bön texts still exist in the modern languages of Kinnaur, Lahul, Spiti, Ladakh, Zanskar, and some Himalayan regions of Nepal.

The Zhang Zhung language had three different scripts, referred to as the wild (dag yig), small (mar yig chungwa), and big (mar yig chewa) scripts. Tibetan script was derived from the Zhang Zhung mar yig scripts. Many Tibetan and western scholars believe that there was no written language before the time of Songtsen Gampo, the king of Tibet in the seventh century A.D. Bön scholars do not accept this view, holding that its proponents have not adequately researched the early origins of the Tibetan language and the history of Tibet.

During his original trip to Tibet, Tönpa Shenrab mainly taught the causal teachings of Bön, because he found that the Tibetans were not ready to receive the higher teachings. At that time, Tönpa Shenrab prophesied that there would come a time when the nine levels of the Bön teachings would be given throughout Tibet.

In the tenth century B.C., many Bön teachings were translated from the Zhang Zhung language into Tibetan by the "Four Great Scholars" (Khepa Mi Zhi): Tong Gyung Thu Chen of Zhang Zhung, Shari Wuchen of Tibet, Gyim Tsa Ma Chung of De, and Chetsa Kharwu of Menyak. Their translations of these teachings, which spread throughout Tibet, are still practiced today. In approximately 1075 B.C., the secret or fruition teachings began to spread more widely, especially during the reign of Mutri Tsenpo, the second king of Tibet, who received these teaching from Namkha Nangwa Dhok Cen of Tagzig.

King Mutri Tsenpo was a great practitioner and master of Bön, and most Bön lineages of the esoteric teachings passed through him. This demonstrates that there was already a rich and developed Tibetan literature at that time. For this reason, Bönpos believe that Tibetan culture did not begin in the seventh century A.D., because teaching and translation from the Zhang Zhung language could not have taken place without first having a language to translate into.

Buddhists first came to Tibet from India at the middle of the seventh century A.D. The spread of Buddhism resulted in the decline of the native Tibetan culture and religion, Bön. The first persecutions of Bönpos began in approximately A.D. 684, during the reign of Drigum Tsenpo, the seventh king of Tibet. The second persecution of Bönpos was during the eighth century, during the reign of Trisong Dewutsen, the thirty-seventh king of Tibet. Many Bön texts and spiritual places were damaged or destroyed during these two periods, and many Bönpos faced great adversity. Bön practitioners were typically given the choice of converting from Bön to Buddhism, leaving Tibet, or being put to death.

THE HIDDEN TREASURES OF BÖN

As these persecutions began, Bön masters (Bön Shen Rigzin) had great concern for the Bön teachings and for the suffering of all sentient beings. Therefore, they hid many of the Bön texts in order to preserve them. They entrusted these texts with prayers and invoked an oath from particular protectors that the texts would be protected until the time was right for them to be rediscovered. These texts are referred to as "hidden treasures" (Bön ter). Later, in the eleventh century, the great treasure revealer Tertön Chenpo, also known as Shen Chen Luga (A.D. 969–1035), and others recovered many of these hidden treasures of Bön. These rediscovered texts are referred to as "terma." Shen Chen Luga systemized these Bön teachings and spread them to his disciples. Once again, the sun of the Bön teachings shone over Tibet.

Shen Chen Luga had many disciples, but three of them are considered his main successors. The first is Dru Je Yungdrung Lama, who established the Yeru Wensa Kha monastery in A.D. 1012 in the Tsang Province of Tibet. Yeru Wensa Kha became a center of Bön education. Druchen Namkha Yungdrung also systemized the methods of philosophical training known as Gap Pa (teaching of Dzogchen), Dzö (teaching of cosmology), and Sa Lam (the stage and paths according to Dho). This center attracted students as a flowers attracts bees and produced many great scholars, including those known as the "Eighteen Great Teachers" (Yeru Tönpa Chogyed) of Wensa Kha.

The second disciple, Zhu Ye Legpo, established the seat of the Zhu lineage in Kyid Khar Rizhing, also in the Tsang Province of Tibet. There he built a monastery and primarily spread the Dzogchen teachings. Lineage holders of this tradition are still alive in Nepal and Tibet.

The third disciple, Patön Palchok Zangpo, was the holder of the Pa lineage and spread the teachings of the Tantric tradition. The monasteries of this lineage were re-established at Hor in the Kham region of Tibet, where the lineage holders of this tradition still live.

In A.D. 1052 the great master and scholar of the Meu lineage, Khepa Palchen, established Zang Ri Meu Tsang Monastery in central Tibet. He also systemized the Bön educational institution. Other monasteries were established throughout Tibet, and the traditions of the Bön teachings and practices were revitalized.

Yeru Wensa Kha Monastery, the main Bön monastery of its time, was destroyed by flood and landslide. In order to preserve the Bön traditions for the benefit of all sentient beings, Nyamed Sherab Gyaltsen (1356–1415) was guided by oral transmissions from Sidpa Gyalmo (the chief protector of Bön) in 1405 to establish a new monastery, Tashi Menri Ling, in the Tobgyal village of Tsang Province. This was considered a miracle, because the monastery was built not only by human hands but also by the protectors, while Nyamed Sherab Gyaltsen was in meditation. He reestablished the teaching tradition of the Dru lineage of Yeru Wensa Kha and attracted many students from all over Tibet. Since then, Menri monastery has become known as the "mother monastery" of all Bönpos.

Menri Monastery follows the monastic rules (cha yig) established by Nyamed Sherab Gyaltsen. According to these rules, a monk's family, wealth, or political position is not considered. The monastery hierarchy is based on seniority (i.e., those who have been monks longer have greater seniority).

Other Bön monasteries and teaching centers were also established. These included Khyung Lung Ngari in Zhang Zhung or upper Tibet and others in Tewa, Jadur, Hor, Tsang, Khyungpo, Derge, Ling Tsang, Menyak, Lithang, Nyagrong, Amdo, and Gayrong. In A.D. 1834 Yungdrung Ling was established by Nang Tön Dawa Gyaltsen (1796–1863) and it eventually became the second most important Bön monastery.

Until 1959 there were three Bön monasteries that functioned as the primary training institutes for monks. These three, Menri, Kharna, and Yungdrung Ling, were referred to as the "upper, middle, and lower land of monks" (Drasa Gong Wog Bar Sum).

Bön and its followers suffered the same fate as other Tibetan religions when the Chinese annexed Tibet in 1959. Many Bön monks and laypersons went into exile in India and Nepal. In 1963 His Holiness the 32nd Menri Trizin, Sherab Lodö, the spiritual leader of the Bön religion and the Abbot of Menri Monastery, passed away in exile in India.

In order to keep the Bönpo community and its culture intact, in 1967 H.E. Yongzin Tenzin Namdak Rinpoche established the "New Tobgyal Bönpo Settlement" of Dolanji, in the Himachal Pradesh region of northern India.

The spiritual leaders of the Bön religion, all now in exile, met in 1969 and performed a traditional ceremony to choose a new throne-holder for Menri Monastery. These leaders included H.H. Sherab Tenpa Gyaltsen (the Abbot of Yungdrung Ling Monastery), Senior Menri Lopon H.E. Sangye Tenzin Rinpoche, H.E. Yongzin Tenzin Namdak Rinpoche, and other lamas, monks, and tulkus. Geshe Sangye Tenzin Jongdong was selected by the protectors as His Holiness the 33rd Menri Trizin, the spiritual leader of Bön.

Since the enthronement of the 33rd H.H. Menri Trizin, a new temple has been built in Dolanji. In addition, Tibetan and English libraries have been established, as well as the central Yungdrung Bön Monastic Centre, which has extensive living quarters for monks.

An orphanage was built within the monastery in order to house boys whose families cannot care for them. In 1978 the Bön Dialectic School, which offers the full traditional training of Yeru Wensa Kha and Menri, was established at Menri Monastery. Food, lodging, and other necessities are provided by H.H. Menri Trizin so that the students at the Bön Dialectic School may apply themselves entirely to their education. H.E. Yongzin Tenzin Namdak Rinpoche and the dialectics teacher, Lharam Geshe Yungdrung Namgyal or "Tsön Du Gongphel," take responsibility for all education and training concerns.

In 1986 six monks were graduated from the Bön Dialectic School at Menri, receiving the Geshe degree (equivalent to a Ph.D. from a western university). These were the first monks to receive the Geshe degree while in exile. Since then, more than fifty Geshes have been graduated from the Bön Dialectic School. Many of them are serving in their native regions to spread the Bön teachings, some travel to the west and spread the Bön teachings, while others remain at Menri monastery. The ancient lineage of the Bön religion is now reestablished and is being passed on to the next generation. Bönpos are proud that their traditions, which have survived great adversity over the centuries, are still alive and active.

Chapter 2

The Proper Way to Receive the Bön Teachings

To develop inner awareness and wisdom, it is necessary to develop the right view toward the teachings. This will not be possible if the practitioner has a wrong attitude about the teachings. Before learning the basic teachings or the preliminary practices, one must establish a solid foundation for future growth and a deep understanding of Bön. Without a good and proper foundation, one's practice will not be stable and reliable. Therefore, it is very important to start with a good understanding of the basics of proper practice.

PURE ATTITUDE OF TEACHER AND STUDENT

Before receiving the teachings, it is essential to prepare oneself by having a pure attitude (motivation) and genuine compassion from the heart.

As an example, in order for a farmer to expect a good crop, it is important to have fertilized the soil. When there is good soil, one can plant and things will grow. If the soil is not good, then whatever one plants will not grow. In the same way, the student's motivation has to

19

be very pure and proper in order to increase positive energy, understand the wisdom of the teachings, and benefit all sentient beings.

There are two necessary attitudes or motivations: the pure attitude of the enlightened ones (jangchup semkyi kunlong), and the Tantric way to purify one's views (nangwa dakpar jawa sangwa ngagkyi kunlong).

Pure Attitude of the Enlightened Ones

Both teacher and student need to have the pure attitude of the enlightened ones. It is important to look within and consider whether one wishes to receive the teachings in order to achieve worldly fame and reputation, gain higher rebirth in the god realms due to fear of suffering in the three lower realms, or liberate oneself only from this cyclic existence of suffering. Wishing to liberate only oneself (thegmen gyi kunlong) is considered to be the lowest level of these incorrect attitudes.

If you have any of these wrong or negative attitudes, you must transform and correct them first by thinking, for instance, that "in the short period of this lifetime, it is not worth benefiting only myself. It is essential for me to overcome the suffering of this cyclic world in order to attain enlightenment for the benefit all sentient beings."

It is important to understand that from the very beginning of your past lives until today, all sentient beings have somehow been connected to you as your father or mother. When they were your parents, they took kind and loving care of you — offering you the most delicious food, covering you with the softest clothes — just as your present parents likely do. Because you have been a child of all of these sentient beings, it is important to realize that you have a responsibility to lead and liberate them from the suffering of this existing world. All sentient beings dislike suffering, but each negative action of their body, mind, and speech cultivates more causes of suffering. Without realizing it, they follow the wrong path and thus experience endless suffering. They do not have the knowledge they need to practice the teachings, so they cannot be liberated from this condition without help.

Therefore, it is essential to generate positive thoughts toward all sentient beings by thinking that they must be liberated and freed from all their negative karmas. To do this, one needs to receive the teachings and commit to one's practice with the goal of achieving enlightenment. We call this "embodying the attitude of enlightenment."

The teacher needs to have a positive motivation for giving the teachings. He should teach in order to benefit his students and all sentient beings. The teachings will not be effective if the teacher does not have this attitude. A quotation from *Drime Zijid*, one of the largest biographies of Tönpa Shenrab, says "Without compassion and the right attitude to giving the teachings in order to benefit the disciples and all sentient beings, it is rather like a donkey wearing a tiger skin to look like a tiger."

The three essential qualities of a teacher include having trust and devotion toward his own teacher and past lineage masters, having compassion for all sentient beings, and having perfect knowledge of Bön. Without trust and devotion to the lineage masters and his root teacher, he will not be blessed by his teachers and past lamas. With these qualities, he will have the blessing and power to help his students detach themselves from the suffering of samsara.

It is also important that the teacher have compassion and a good attitude toward the teachings. For example, the great hermit Gongzod Ritöd Chenpo always did prayers and requested blessings by first repeating the name of his teacher, such as "Jetsun Trotsang La" and "Jetsun Jangpa La." Only then did he start the teachings.

If a teacher lacks compassion for sentient beings, he will not have the ability to generate the good will necessary to benefit students and others by his teachings. If he is seeking only fame and reputation, he will be unable to guide his students on the pathway to enlightenment.

Without perfect knowledge of Bön in general, and of his special topic of expertise in particular, the teacher may not be able to properly interpret the meaning of the teachings. If students do not receive the teachings with the correct attitude and understanding that are essential for developing their practice, then they will not achieve realization.

The Tantric Way of Purifying One's Views

The second important attitude is the Tantric way of purifying one's views, which means to transform one's ordinary and dualistic views and conceptions into a higher spiritual vision.

For instance, you transform the place where teachings are received from an ordinary classroom into a complete and perfected mandala of the deities. You view the teacher as a pure form of Shen Lha Ökar, the Buddha of Compassion, by mentally transforming him from an ordinary person into an enlightened one who has manifested in a human body to guide all sentient beings. You transform your companions and classmates from ordinary beings into deities and goddesses, and believe that they all have love, compassion, and care for all sentient beings.

The purpose of transforming your views into pure visions toward these objects is to realize the extraordinary nature of this experience. This gives you a special reason to receive blessings and powers from the teacher (lama), the enlightened ones (Sangye), the deities (yidam), and the female manifestations of the enlightened ones (khadro), in order to develop your wisdom and stability. This is the essence of the practice of purifying one's view according to the Tantric ways.

To achieve maximum benefit, the practitioner must generate both the motivation of the enlightened one and the motivation of the secret Sang Ngag. Before receiving teachings, doing practices, and receiving empowerment or oral transmission, the student should start his practice each time with these motivations, so that the benefits of the practice will be multiplied.

Pure motivation provides the student with good conditions for the teachings to take root and blossom into enlightenment. If you lack pure motivation, then impure and deluded thoughts may destroy any good results of your practice. It is important to correct and purify any improper attitudes and motives.

PROPER MOTIVATION OF STUDENTS

The essence of the Bön teachings is based on compassion, love, nonviolence, and kindness. If you practice accordingly, you will obtain a better understanding of your own nature, and the nature of all phenomena.

In other words, the ultimate goal of practice is to discover your natural state of mind and to achieve enlightenment. Discovering your true nature is essential to purifying your negative thoughts, which are influenced by the five poisons: anger, attachment, ignorance, jealousy, and pride. The ability to generate pure thoughts helps you to be of benefit to other sentient beings and gives a meaningful purpose to your life.

As an example, we can be like a lotus flower, which is beautiful even though it is growing in the mud. Its beauty is never affected by its surroundings. As we are born into the miserable conditions of this cyclic existence, we need to emphasize how to overcome or free ourselves from suffering. By applying the teachings to our everyday practice, we are not affected by the poisons of this world.

The teachings of Bön are like a mirror that is able to reflect the appearance of objects. In the same way, through practice, you will be able to notice and realize the influence of negative thoughts and the five poisons, and therefore mindfully control and subdue them. Use the practice as a mirror to reflect your inner self. The more you are able to overcome or subdue negative thoughts, the more you will improve your understanding and the level of your practice.

QUALITIES REQUIRED OF STUDENTS

Two sets of characteristics are required of practitioners: qualities to avoid (the three faults of the container and the nine faults to avoid), and qualities to achieve (the knowledge of holding, the knowledge of understanding, and the knowledge of realization).

Qualities to Avoid

Three Faults of the Container

The three faults that each student should avoid, known as "the three faults of the container," are being like an upside-down container, being like a container with a hole in the bottom, or being like a container with poison inside.

1. Being like an upside-down container, symbolized by a pot that is upside down

When you are a disciple listening to the teachings, your consciousness has to be focused on what the teacher is saying, so that you hear every word the teacher says. If instead your consciousness is focused elsewhere, no matter how many valuable teachings you receive, you will be like a pot that is held upside down under a water tap; no matter how much water flows over it, no water will remain inside.

The presence of your physical body is not sufficient to fulfill the purpose of receiving the teachings. Although you are hearing the sound of the teacher's voice, you become like a cat or dog in the classroom who can hear the sounds of the Bön teaching, but can never understand the meaning of the words.

2. Being like a container with a hole in the bottom, symbolized by a pot with a hole in its bottom

It is important to remember what you hear with clear awareness, and not to forget what you have heard of the teachings.

25

Apply the teachings to your practice and your day-to-day life, and avoid the negative actions of body, mind, and speech, as these are the sources of all suffering. If you are not able to remember the teachings and their essence, you are lacking the right focus. If your consciousness is completely distracted by endless projections of past, present, or future plans, then your mind is like a pot with a hole in the bottom; no matter how much water flows in, no water will remain in the pot. In other words, no matter how much you hear, nothing will remain in your mind to practice because you are distracted. You have to receive the teachings with your full attention.

3. Being like a container with poison inside, symbolized by a pot with poison in it

It is important to receive the teachings with a pure attitude so that you can benefit all sentient beings. If you listen to the teachings under the influence of any of the five poisons, your mind is like a pot with poison; no matter how much delicious food is contained in the pot, none can be eaten.

It is *essential* that the student clearly focuses on what the teacher says — the essence of the teaching — then keeps this essence in mind in order to reflect on it during practice and thereby gain realization. If you generate any of the five poisons while attending a teaching, because you are under the influence of that poison, the teaching (despite its great value) will not bring about a positive result toward achieving your realization and further developing your wisdom.

In conclusion, these three faults are the main obstructions to receiving the teachings, practicing them, and applying them toward achieving realization. It is very important to realize the interconnectedness of receiving the teachings through the ear consciousness, holding their essence in the mind consciousness without forgetting, and practicing their essence. Integrating this practice in your life every day will make life better, happier, and more meaningful.

Nine Faults to Avoid

According to the *Dzogchen Yang Tse Longchen*, there are nine faults to be avoided by Bön practitioners: distrusting the Bön teachings, disrespecting the teacher, lacking commitment to your practice, wasting the essence of the teaching by not practicing, not valuing the practice, postponing your practice because of family or other responsibilities, being distracted (the distractions of consciousness), lacking clarity in practice, and feeling sadness or disappointment because of long practice sessions or teachings.

1. Distrusting the Bön Teachings   Not trusting the Bön teachings will automatically block your ability to enter the pathway of enlightenment. You will not receive power and blessings from the Three Jewels (Könchog Sum), the enlightened ones (Sangye), the Bön teachings (the teachings of Tönpa Shenrab), or the great masters who have achieved realization and have generated the mind of enlightenment (Yungdrung Sempa). It is as if you have two amputated legs and will not be able to go from one place to another without the help of someone you trust. Likewise, if you do not trust your teacher, even though he has great powers and blessings to give, you will not be able to receive those blessings. When you practice in order to achieve enlightenment, one of the most essential things you need is trust and faith in the teachings and the teacher. Only this trust and faith will open the door to the teachings.

Trust is equally necessary for everyone. If you generate trust within yourself, you will have a good basis for your practice. It will be like the glue that you can use to adhere the essence of the teachings to your mindstream. Trust is the source of all these qualities.

2. Disrespecting the Teacher If you do not have respect toward the teacher, who is the source of your knowledge and wisdom, it will be impossible for you to achieve enlightenment, even though the Bön teachings are the root source of the achievement of enlightenment. Nothing will enable you to do this without receiving instructions and guidance from the teacher. If you do not view your teacher as a real form of Shen Lha Ökar, the Buddha of Compassion, then you will not be able to receive his knowledge and blessings.

A student once asked the great Dzogchen master known as Gyer Pung Nang Zher Löd Po, "What is the most important quality needed to receive the essence of the teacher?" The answer was, "The blessings from the teacher." Again, the student raised the question, "What is most important for receiving the blessings?" The answer was, "To see and view the teacher as having completely achieved wisdom and compassion, as being always with you, and as watching and surrounding you always with the truth of the teachings and the blessings of the Enlightened Ones of the Ten Directions (Chok Chu Sangye)." This is true, even if the teacher himself is not well qualified.

As an illustration of this, there is a story of a hermit who lived in the forest in early times. Several fishermen in a nearby village suffered through a difficult period in which fish, food, and even clothes were lacking. The fishermen were completely exhausted by this difficult situation. One day, on their way home, they saw the hermit, who was behaving in a very pleasant and happy manner. They felt inspired by his way of living and decided to devote themselves to receiving teachings from him and renouncing worldly life. They went to offer him all their fishing nets and hunting equipment. With complete trust and devotion, they asked him to accept them as his students and give them teachings so that they could achieve enlightenment. The hermit was not qualified to give such teachings, but he did not want to admit that to the fishermen. Therefore, he taught them in a very negative manner. He asked them: "Are you able to trust me completely and do whatever I ask of you?" They replied: "Absolutely! We are waiting for your instructions and will do everything you ask of us." Then the hermit said: "All of you must hold hands and jump from here down to the lake." The fishermen thought this was a method for teaching very sinful persons, such as fishermen and hunters, how to achieve liberation, so without any doubts they jumped. Before they fell into the lake they were all lifted up by an eagle, who was actually a manifestation of the Enlightened Ones of the Ten Directions, and they achieved enlightenment.

This is good example of the necessity of generating complete trust and faith in the teacher so that the blessings and power of the enlightened ones are always with you. The truth of the teachings of Tönpa Shenrab led to the fishermen's enlightenment, not the wrong teachings of the hermit.

Afterward, the hermit was very proud that the fishermen had achieved liberation. He mistakenly thought that this had been caused by his guidance. He was sure that he could achieve liberation as the fishermen had, so he jumped from his cave to the lake below and was killed.

This is symbolic of the result of negative thoughts. Strong blessings and power can appear according to the strength of your own faith. What you receive is dependent on how much trust you have toward the teacher and the teachings.

3. Lacking Commitment to Your Practice   If you lack commitment to your practice, it will be easy to interrupt the continuity of your practice, even though the teacher has shown you the suffering caused by committing nonvirtuous deeds and the importance of avoiding those actions.

By doing your practice, you will develop the inspiration for good deeds. Therefore, it is important to make a commitment to your practice so that you can reach your ultimate goal. We have to commit ourselves to do practice on a regular basis, every day of our lives. For instance, one can commit to reciting one of the essential recitations three hundred times every day, or to meditating for fifteen minutes every day.

Even if you have some interest in the teachings and practice because of your teacher or your spiritual friends, without commitment, your interest will gradually decrease and deluded dualistic thinking will easily interfere with that practice. Slowly, you will lose your faith and become engaged in activities that will keep you in this cyclic world.

You should also make a commitment to avoid nonvirtuous deeds of body, mind, and speech. Do this step by step and choose goals. Resolve to yourself in this way: "Tomorrow I will not generate anger or jealousy toward anyone."

It is important that you are completely aware of your commitment to practice. Gradually you will develop the wisdom and power to overcome suffering and its sources, and achieve enlightenment.

4. Wasting the Essence of the Teachings by Not Practicing   If you are receiving the teachings without practicing, after some time you will lose interest in what you have received. If you do not appreciate the value of the teachings, there will be no accomplishment of the goal.

When you are hungry and have a full plate of food in front of you, you have to make an effort to put it into your mouth. The food will not come into your mouth by itself, and you will remain hungry if you do not make the effort to eat. In the same way, if you do not apply the teachings by practicing, there will not be any chance to achieve the ultimate goal.

It is essential to have an interest in the practice. Whoever has that interest will achieve realization through practice. When seriously seeking to achieve the ultimate goal, the amount of time it takes is not important. In Tibet there is a saying, "The teachings are a kind of jewel that do not belong to any one person, but will come to the one who is enthusiastic about the teachings and committed to practicing."

5. Not Valuing the Practice   When you do not realize the value of the teachings and lack a strong desire to practice, you will more easily postpone your practice until tomorrow or next week or next month. Having postponed the practice, you will die before achieving any results.

Therefore, it is important to realize what a wonderful opportunity it is to meet a teacher and receive teachings. Generate thoughts that lead you to practice more actively and meaningfully.

When you experience the moment of death, do not be in a position to regret that you did not practice when there was still time to practice. Prepare yourself during your lifetime so that when the time comes you will be able to follow the path of dying with confidence in your own practice.

6. Postponing Your Practice Because of Family or Other Responsibilities   If you want to be a serious and dedicated practitioner and you are tired of this worldly life, your practice must not depend on any conditions or circumstances such as family, friends, or other people. It is important to make your decision freely without pressure from anyone.

Continually remember all the qualities of the enlightened ones and understand the power of the practices to overcome suffering. Try to keep in mind the following thought: "Today I will remember every word the teacher says, reflect on their meaning, and integrate them into my practice. I must achieve enlightenment right in this session."

If you do not waste any time, you will benefit from every moment of doing the practice.

7. Being Distracted (the Distractions of Consciousness) When your mind begins to produce limitless thoughts and becomes distracted by the six objects of consciousness, you will be led far from the essence of the teachings and the five poisons will be activated. Therefore, it is necessary to stabilize your mind and focus more gently and precisely on the teachings.

The six objects or distractions of consciousness are:
1. eye consciousness, or distraction by objects;
2. ear consciousness, or distraction by sounds;
3. nose consciousness, or distraction by smell;
4. tongue consciousness, or distraction by taste;
5. body consciousness, or distraction by feeling;
6. mind consciousness, or distraction by limitless arising thoughts of past, present, and future.

8. Lacking Clarity in Your Practice By producing limitless thoughts of the past, present, and future, and following these thoughts so that you completely lose your concentration on the teachings, you have begun what is known as a main hindrance to normalizing your state of mind. It is important to recognize the wildness of your thoughts and learn how to stabilize them. While being aware of the risk of distraction, try to keep your concentration focused on the teachings.

9. Feeling Disappointment Because of Long Practice Sessions or Teachings   Rather than being frustrated by the length of the practice sessions and other factors, realize how lucky your circumstances are and how rare it is to have a perfect human body. It is also important to realize your good fortune of meeting the teacher and having an opportunity to receive the teachings. This chance is not given to everyone. Therefore, receive the teachings and do your practice with joy and enthusiasm, and with the intention to achieve enlightenment within this lifetime.

Qualities to Achieve

There are three primary qualities of practice to be cultivated by students as follows.

The Knowledge of Holding (Zinpi Lo)

This knowledge is like glue. Whatever it touches, it holds without releasing. Students need to have the knowledge that holds all the teachings. Firstly, hold the words of the teachings; secondly, hold these words without forgetting them; and thirdly, keep their meaning in mind.

The Knowledge of Understanding (Bardu Togpi Lo)

This knowledge involves distinguishing the positive from the negative — knowing what should be kept and what should be discarded — as a gold miner keeps the gold nuggets and throws away the mud. In this way, students have the knowledge to distinguish the virtuous qualities of the enlightened ones from the nonvirtue of this cyclic world.

The Knowledge of Realization (Togpi Lo)

This knowledge allows students to make distinctions even among virtuous things, to be able to differentiate between the precious jewels and the gold. In this way, an understanding of the various teachings of Tönpa Shenrab and the ability meditate on the true nature of mind without interruption can arise. In addition, one can practice the Ten Transcendental Practices (Parchin Chu).

QUALITIES TO BE CULTIVATED BY THE TEACHER

In order to achieve enlightenment, we need to practice meditation. In order to meditate, we need to realize the nature of our mind. To realize the nature of our mind, it is important to have instruction and guidance from a teacher. There is no history of achieving enlightenment without following a teacher.

Without a guide, a person who does not know a particular country cannot make a proper decision about where to go. In the same way, we sentient beings have no knowledge of how to enter the path of enlightenment without a teacher. In the past, the great masters, scholars, and translators of Zhang Zhung and Tibet followed their teachers' instructions and achieved enlightenment. In the eighth century the great master Denpa Namkha followed 108 teachers to achieve enlightenment. We sentient beings need to have a qualified teacher who can guide us and tell us what to do and what to avoid.

It is important to find a qualified Bön teacher who has received the transmission of the Bön teachings through an unbroken lineage and can lead us in the right direction. He must have knowledge of the Bön teachings in general, and have his own experience of realization of the nature of mind through meditation. He must also be fluent in the particular subject he is teaching and have the wisdom and knowledge to guide his students. Without discriminating among his students, he needs to be enthusiastic about teaching them tirelessly for the benefit of all sentient beings.

It is important for Bön teachers to embody the following six qualities:

1. he must have *realized the true nature of mind,*
2. he must have the *experience of perfect contemplation* in the state of meditation,
3. his character and behavior must be in accordance with the teachings so that he is an *example to all sentient beings,*
4. he must have *attained complete realization* of the stages and the path to enlightenment,
5. he must be *detached from the material world* and apply all his energies to achieving enlightenment, and
6. he must *always be engaged in the practice and teaching of Bön.*

If the teacher does not have faith and trust in his lineage and his own teachers, he will have no blessings to offer his students. If he is lacking in compassion toward his students and all sentient beings, his teaching will not bring good results, and he will be unable to point his students in the direction of enlightenment. If he lacks knowledge of the particular subject he is teaching, he will not be able to help his disciples understand that subject. He will not open his disciples' minds to an understanding of the true quality of wisdom. Thus, attending his teachings will be a waste of time.

The teacher himself must pray and generate pure motivation to teach, to receive blessings from his masters and lineage, and to liberate all sentient beings by giving the teachings.

While these instructions are not exhaustive, they provide general guidelines for practitioners and teachers. One detail is especially important: *once a practitioner has decided to follow a teacher, the student should never, through his or her limited knowledge, question or judge the value of the teacher.* The student should consider the teacher only as pure and perfect.

Chapter 3

Fourfold Practices to Train One's Mind

To better understand the Bön teachings and their qualities, it is important to realize the value of one's perfect human birth together with its nature of impermanence. As long as we have not achieved enlightenment, we will perpetually be in this cyclic world of suffering, complaint, and disappointment. We will experience the results of our actions according to our own deeds — both positive and negative. To overcome suffering, we need to understand and realize the law of cause and result.

The Fourfold Practices (Lodhog Namzhi) used to tame the untrained mind according to Bön are as follows:

- Realizing the Rareness of a Perfect Human Body
  (Daljor Nyed Kawa),
- Realizing the Nature of the Impermanence of Life
  (Tse Mi Tagpa),
- Realizing the Sources of Suffering in this Cyclic World
  (Khorwai Nyemig), and
- Understanding the Law of Cause and Result
  (Le Gyu Dre).

REALIZING THE RARENESS OF A
PERFECT HUMAN BODY

First, what does it mean to have realized the rareness of a perfect human body? We need to determine whether or not we have perfected the eighteen qualities that make a perfect human body. The eighteen perfected qualities (yönten chogyed) are the eight conditions (dalwa gyed) and the ten perfections (jorwa chu).

If you have not perfected these qualities, then you must practice and find a way to achieve them. Imperfection in even one of these qualities will make a difference in your practice. If you have achieved all of these qualities, it is very important to honor them by making a commitment to use this rare opportunity in this lifetime to engage in practice and to help all sentient beings.

The Eight Conditions

In order to perfect the eight qualities, firstly, you must not live in any of the following eight conditions. This is because their respective sufferings will interfere with your practice.

1. The Hell Realm One is born in the hell realm due to one's anger in past lives. In the hell realm, one is constantly suffering from cold and heat. Not one single moment is free from suffering. Therefore, there is no opportunity or time to practice or receive teachings. That is why this realm is not free from suffering.

2. The Hungry Ghost Realm Birth into this realm is caused by attachment. In the hungry ghost realm, there is constant suffering from hunger and thirst. In every moment of their lives, these beings languish for food and drink, but even when they receive it, they are unable to absorb it and continue to suffer. Therefore, they have no ability to practice.

There is a story related to this about Tertön Guru Nontse, a great discoverer of the treasures of Bön and a well-known teacher. In a vision, he asked an elderly hungry ghost lady, "Do you understand the quality of virtuous and nonvirtuous deeds? Do you know any recitation or prayers?" She replied, "I know the qualities of virtuous and nonvirtuous deeds and can recite prayers as well, but many of my five hundred children are dying because of hunger and thirst. There is no moment when I am free to engage in the practice."

3. The Animal Realm Taking birth as any form of animal is caused by ignorance. The sufferings of these beings include nonawakening, no freedom of making decisions, and dependency. Among the animals, the highest form is a domestic animal. If you placed one hundred volumes of Tönpa Shenrab's teachings in front of them and recited the teachings, these animals may receive the blessings of the prayers; otherwise, they cannot understand a single word. Since they are always suffering from lack of clarity and knowledge, they are not free at any moment. Therefore, there is no single moment to engage in even the smallest amount of practice.

4. The Long-Life God Realm Those born in this realm believe they have achieved the ultimate goal and are thus very satisfied with themselves. This is the reason why they do not engage in any kind of practice. They spend most of their lives in a state of nonperception. Immediately before dying, they suddenly realize that there is a possibility that they will be reborn in a lower realm and, at that moment, they generate a wrong view about their achievement. Having no opportunity to practice, there is no chance to change their wrong view toward the teachings, and their suffering will continue.

5. The Absence of the Enlightened Ones   The period of the absence of the enlightened ones is known as the dark eon. Those born into a place where there are no enlightened ones are not fortunate enough to receive the teachings of Bön. Therefore, they will not understand the essence of Bön and also will not be able to distinguish between the qualities of virtuous and nonvirtuous deeds. Every moment of their lives will result in more suffering, and there will be no time or place for practice.

6. The Absence of the Teachings   Those born in a place where the Bön teachings have not been taught due to their karma will certainly not know what and how to practice, nor will they know the value of Bön. They will naturally lack an understanding of the quality of the enlightened ones (Sangye) and of virtuous action. Therefore, there is no chance to achieve enlightenment. They will not be able to gain freedom from the suffering of cyclic existence.

7. Having Imperfect Health Conditions   If you are born as a disabled or mentally disordered person, although you have the opportunity to receive the teachings, you will not be able to understand their essence. For instance, if you are blind, you have no ability to receive blessings by seeing the enlightened ones and the teachers. If you are deaf, there is no chance to hear the words of the teachings. If you are dumb, you cannot recite and discuss the meaning of the teachings. If you are mentally afflicted, then you have no opportunity to apply the teachings to your practice and hence clearly understand virtuous and nonvirtuous deeds as well as the qualities of suffering and enlightenment. You will always suffer from the lack of those qualities.

8. Having Wrong Views Toward the Teaching If you develop wrong views toward the teachings, then you will not be able to practice the teachings in any way. Instead, you will cultivate negative views and bad karma. Lacking positive views toward the teachings, you will cease receiving the blessings, energy, and power of Bön.

These are the eight conditions that will hinder students from practicing freely (mi khom pi ne gyed). Under these conditions, there is no possibility of practicing in order to achieve enlightenment. According to a quotation from the *Dangwa Don Gyi Dho*, "If you are born in any form as a being of the hell, hungry ghost, or animal realms, which are not free from suffering, there is no way to understand the teachings and no chance to receive the teachings. Because of nonunderstanding there is no practice, because of nonpracticing there is no way to achieve enlightenment." One must have the good fortune to be free from all these obstacles in order to practice and gain understanding. Only then is there a way to enter the pathway of enlightenment.

The Ten Perfections

Among the ten perfections (jorwa chu) to be achieved, there are two major categories with five perfections each. The first category has five perfections that are related to one's own condition (rangjor nga) and the second category has five perfections that are related to exterior conditions (zhenjor nga).

The five perfections related to one's own condition are as follows.

• According to the great master Denpa Namkha, the first perfection related to one's own condition is the condition of possessing a perfect human body.

• The second is the condition of being born in a place where it is possible to receive the teachings. The world we live in now (Zambu Div) is a world where we are able to receive the Bön teachings.

• The third is to possess in perfect condition all of the five senses and six consciousnesses that comprise the main physical qualities of a human being.

• The fourth is to have a pure intention toward practice, known as the condition of the capacity of understanding the teachings.

• The fifth is to have complete devotion and trust toward the teachings, and practice what has been learned from the teachings.

The five perfections related to exterior conditions are as follows.

• The first of these perfections is being born during the period when Tönpa Shenrab's manifestation has given teachings. This is known as the condition of the presence of the enlightened one

(Sangye). Without Tönpa Shenrab, there would be no Bön teachings in this eon.

• The second is the promulgation of the Bön teachings. Tönpa Shenrab taught the nine ways of Bön in order to benefit all beings according to their capacity to understand the teachings. Each student is perfected on the condition that the Bön teaching is taught. Even though Tönpa Shenrab is an enlightened being who has been born in this world and has given blessings, if he had not taught Bön, then no one would be able to benefit from the teachings.

• The third is the continued presence of the Bön teachings. If the teachings given by Tönpa Shenrab are lost or naturally disappear, that period would be very similar to one in which there is an absence of the Bön teachings. Thus, this condition is referred to as the condition of the presence of the teachings.

• The fourth is the presence of a teacher with the ability to teach. Even though Bön exists, if you do not meet a teacher who can lead you to the path to enlightenment, you will never benefit and understand its essence. Having the good fortune to meet a qualified teacher and receive instructions from him or her is referred to as the perfection of the instructor.

• The fifth is the compassion of the teacher. Even if you meet a qualified teacher, if he does not accept you as his disciple, or has no compassion or good will with the intention to liberate all sentient beings from the suffering of this cyclic existence, then even if you are surrounded by texts of the Bön teachings, you will not benefit from or fully understand the essence of Bön, nor connect to the lineage of the Bön tradition. Meeting such a teacher is very important for connecting to the lineage and following such a teacher is called the perfection of the compassionate teacher.

All of these eighteen conditions are essential in order to perfect oneself and they depend on one's past lives and past karma. These conditions are not easily achieved; this is done only through the limitless merit that one has earned in previous lifetimes and is now experiencing. It is not certain that one will always achieve a perfect human body and have the opportunity to meet teachers and receive teachings. Therefore, it is extremely important to realize the rareness of this perfect human body and to generate the wish to make this present life meaningful. Whatever we experience — pleasure or pain, happiness or unhappiness — has to do with the law of cause and result.

Eventually we will experience the result of our own deeds. It is our responsibility to practice and achieve realization of the natural state of mind so that we can reach the ultimate goal. Whether or not we cultivate negative actions, and whether or not we are influenced by the five poisons, spending our lifetime with an attitude of self-concern results in endless suffering. If we plant a poisoned tree, the fruit of that tree is certain to be poisonous. We can only overcome all suffering if we cleanse our impurities, cultivate even the smallest merits through prayers, and generate good attitudes toward others. This is following the pathway Tönpa Shenrab has shown us.

In general, you may think that to achieve a human body is not very rare because the population of the world is growing fast. What is referred to here as the rareness of the perfect human body is something very different. It is common to find human beings with one or more of the necessary conditions for enlightenment, but it is extraordinary to find human beings with all eighteen perfected conditions. What is even more rare is to find a human being with all eighteen perfected conditions who is also dedicated to doing practice and benefiting all sentient beings.

It is necessary to apply these qualities to meaningful actions that benefit all sentient beings. According to a quotation from a Dzogchen text, "Do not waste a meaningful life. Rather, prepare to achieve everlasting peace in this present life." Based on our actions and choices, we will experience goodness or suffering. Instead of being proud of having achieved a perfect human body, we can reflect on the rareness of those qualities. It is not certain that we will have a similarly perfect human body in the next life. Everything needs to be accomplished in this lifetime when all these perfected qualities are present. With full awareness, we should devote ourselves completely to the practice with the attitude of achieving enlightenment during this present life. Because our human body is like a bridge between the upper and lower realms, into which realm we are going to be reborn is very much in our own hands.

Therefore, we need to devote every possible moment of our lives to our practice in order to achieve enlightenment within this lifetime. Being distracted by worldly life increases the chances of being born in one of the realms that are full of suffering.

We all should understand clearly from the core of our hearts that this temporary human body is like finding a treasure in a dream — when you wake up from the dream you have nothing in your hands. Likewise, if you fail to apply the teachings to your practice in order to make this present life meaningful, then the purpose of the teachings is not fulfilled. All the sources of peace or suffering rely on this human body. By generating our pure intention toward the teachings and their essence so that we can benefit all sentient beings, we can be liberated from the suffering of cyclic existence.

REALIZING THE NATURE OF THE IMPERMANENCE OF LIFE

It is very important for practitioners to deeply realize the nature of impermanence (tse mi tagpa). The more you understand the nature of impermanence and become familiar with it through practice in your day-to-day life, you will be encouraged to practice regularly without postponement as well, and this will also deepen your understanding of reality.

We all have a general wish to practice, but since we lack true realization of the aspect of impermanence, we postpone our regular practices day after day, week after week. We believe that we will practice the next day or next week because we often think in a very certain way that we will still be here tomorrow or the next day. Actually, it is very uncertain, and we should realize this clearly. The most important thing is to be aware of the rareness of the perfect human body and to reflect on its meaning. If one misses an opportunity, perhaps there will not be another one. This perfected quality is very impermanent and can be taken away at any time due to many conditions or circumstances.

There are six different methods by which to better realize impermanence as follows.

1. Meditate on impermanence by reflecting on the changing and evolving universe. The universe is structured according to the common merit of sentient beings in the form of mountains, lakes, oceans, and so on. Each of these seems very stable and permanent to the human eye, but everything is actually evolving. For instance, erosion can alter bodies of water. Mountains may be changed forever by landslides, volcanic eruptions, earthquakes, and so forth. Fire, wind, rain, and other elements can alter the physical landscape.

2. Meditate on impermanence by reflecting on the condition of sentient beings in the universe and their birth, death, and suffering. In the same way the universe is evolving and being destroyed, the sentient beings contained in this universe are also evolving and disappearing due to the three major crises of sickness, hunger, and war. According to a quotation from one of the *Dho* texts, "None of the sentient beings will last forever without changing or dying." We all agree that because we have been born, the end of our life is death. But we do not really realize it from deep within as an experience of impermanence. In the six realms of existence, from the beginning until now, none of our ancestors has lived forever. They all followed the path of impermanence and died from different conditions, such as hunger, sickness, or war. Tönpa Shenrab and the great enlightened ones who manifested in human form have shown us the pathway of death and transformation so that we can understand the true quality of impermanence.

3. Meditate on impermanence by reflecting on the nature of the death and birth of the great enlightened ones and masters of the past. The reason we take the great masters and enlightened ones as examples is to realize that if they had to die, there can be no chance for a normal sentient being to live forever. Those great masters of Zhang Zhung and Tibet who empowered themselves to manifest during any time went through the process of death. They all followed the same path of dying, which emphasizes that we sentient beings should also be prepared to follow the pathway of impermanence and give up our conception that life is permanent.

4. Meditate on impermanence by reflecting on the birth and death of sentient beings. All beings, from the highest levels of the god realms to the lowest level of the hell realms, have passed away. A quotation from a Sang Ngag text says, "After your birth there is no other path to follow than the pathway of death and no way to escape from the rule of the lord of death."

There are always lessons to learn about impermanence. If you reflect on the period of your present life from your birth until now, many of your relatives, neighbors, and friends from childhood through youth to old age have suffered sickness and death. From the most powerful people of the world to the poorest, everyone must follow the same pathway and everyone is equally limited by the nature of impermanence. If you reflect on this, you can apply it to your day-to-day life so that you will have a greater understanding of the nature and qualities of impermanence. When the time comes for you to die, you can face death without regret and agitation. You will be able to follow the pathway of wisdom and more easily achieve enlightenment due to your experience of practice. If you are mindful, there are many aspects of your daily life and surroundings that will improve your realization of the impermanence of life.

5. Meditate on impermanence by reflecting on various examples of transformations. Think about the gradual changes within the seasons. Think about moments when you feel pleasure and how that same feeling can be transformed into sadness simply because of the way nature changes. You can also think of changes in the lives of individuals. For example, good relationships among families and friends can suddenly change into angry and violent ones. Perhaps someone you dislike and think of as an enemy will suddenly become a good friend. Your health may suddenly be transformed by an illness. There are limitless examples in your daily life and surroundings that demonstrate the real impermanence of life.

6. Meditate on impermanence by reflecting on the experience of death. We sentient beings expect that we will live for a long time, without remembering that death can occur at any time and any place, and under any circumstances. Because we lack an understanding of the true nature of uncertainty, we have the conception that since we are young and healthy, and have a family history of long life, we will live for a long time. This conception is the main obstacle to realizing the true nature of impermanence. We may not have the same long life as other family members have had because everyone has his or her own karma and destiny. Death can happen at any moment, and we will have no choice except to follow that pathway.

When death comes there is no way for you or your family to

save your life or postpone your death. The only help available is through your virtuous deeds, your trust and faith in the enlightened ones, your teacher, and the teachings (and their blessings), and your practice. Everything else in your life consists only of material objects that hinder you and cause attachment to your life. These things will obstruct your pathway to enlightenment.

It is important to meditate on impermanence in order to detach yourself from the suffering of this cyclic world and to develop the wisdom of realization. This will allow you to attain enlightenment. Having only an understanding of impermanence is not sufficient to achieve enlightenment. It is essential to realize that every single moment of your life can be influenced by practice. Only in this way can self-centeredness and grasping be overcome.

Following the examples of former masters can inspire your practice on impermanence. In earlier times the great masters in Tibet often went to a cemetery to meditate. This is a good place to experience the impermanence of life. Some practitioners have even hung a skeleton on their door to remind themselves that the skeleton was once part of a human body, but its state was changed because of the nature of impermanence.

REALIZING THE SOURCES OF SUFFERING IN THIS CYCLIC WORLD

It is not enough to understand the precious quality of your human birth. It is more essential to realize the sources of suffering in cyclic existence (khorwai nyemig) and to apply this realization to your practice. This will help you overcome the ocean of suffering forever.

If you do not realize the true sources of suffering, there is no way to completely free yourself.

Once there is birth, there is also death. Where there is death, birth will come again. Rebirth will take place repeatedly in one of the six realms until enlightenment is achieved. This is why it is referred to as the cyclic world (khorwa). Once you have taken birth in cyclic existence according to the karmic deeds of your past lives, you will experience those fruits in this present life. This condition is not beyond suffering.

In order to liberate yourself from suffering you need to make a commitment to achieve enlightenment. To overcome suffering you must first realize the source and nature of suffering. This realization gives you an opportunity to avoid the causes of suffering.

The most common sources of suffering experienced by all human beings are:

- suffering of the four faults (birth, old age, sickness, and death),
- suffering of fear,
- suffering caused by worry about the possibility of separation from loved ones,
- suffering of a lack of basic needs, and
- suffering of the fear of loss of your wealth.

Suffering of the Four Faults

1. Suffering of Birth (Kyewe Dhug Ngal)

As we are human beings, the very beginning of our life always takes place in the warmth of our mother's body. Our suffering begins there. When your mother sleeps, you feel pressure as though you were under a huge mountain. When your mother moves, it is like "riding a wild horse." When your mother eats hot or cold food, you have the experience of suffering from hot or cold. When you are about to enter this world, you experience the suffering of birth whether you remember it or not. That is the beginning of suffering in this lifetime.

2. Suffering of Old Age (Gepi Dhug Ngal)

As you move through the endless activities of this cyclic existence, one after another like the waves of the ocean, you end up at the period of old age. Wrinkles appear on your face, your hair turns gray, and your teeth begin to fall out. Suddenly you need the support of a stick to stand up and sit down. You lose your taste for food and your ability to walk, and you experience unsteadiness. This is the suffering we will experience as we near the end of your life. All these changes provide us with lessons in understanding and preparing for a better next life. We need to realize this and integrate this understanding in our practice.

3. Suffering of Sickness (Nawe Dhug Ngal)

Our material bodies depend on the physical conditions of inner and external elements such as food, clothes, accommodations, etc. Pollution by inner and outer poisons causes sicknesses of wind/breath (lung), bile (tripa), and mucus (peken). The effect of sickness will be visible on our skin and in our behavior and character. The malfunction of our inner organs causes tremendous suffering, which decreases the energy of our body, the vibration of our voice, and the look of our face. Gradually this will push us toward the end of our life. The suffering of our physical body is like a fish dropped onto the sand; our mind becomes like a wild animal caught in a trap. This happens to all be-ings. The only way to face this suffering in a more flexible way is to realize the nature of the gradual changes in your life.

4. Suffering of Death (Chiwe Dhug Ngal)

Depending on your karma, there are different ways to experience the suffering of death. Some people are calm and ready to die. Others are very agitated and afraid of death, not knowing the way of dying and the nature of death. At the moment of death your relatives and friends surround you. You are suffering at that moment because you are attached to your relatives and the wealth built up during your life-time. You are not able to talk and you suffer from agitation and worry. At that moment you may regret the lack of practice that is the only way to be released from the suffering of death. Regret at that last moment does not help you overcome suffering because it is too late.

Therefore, it is important to be prepared in time so that we will be able to follow the path of dying more peacefully. For that we must develop a clear understanding of the nature of death, while we still have energy and time. It is essential to always remember your practice, your teacher, and the teachings of the great masters of the past. Pray to these masters and seek their blessings so that you can be protected from the suffering of death and be able to achieve enlightenment.

Suffering of Fear

All sentient beings experience suffering from fear (dra dang te dod kyi dhug ngal) on different levels. For example, by possessing material things, we accumulate wealth and property. With each acquisition, we expect to attain more joy and happiness. Instead, we add more suffering by worrying about their protection. The fear of losing the objects of wealth through robbery or damage will chase you your whole life. Therefore, it is best to free yourself from this suffering of fear by doing everything you can for good causes, such as the generous use of your wealth to benefit others. This means giving money and assets to charitable organizations, such as those with needy children, so that others benefit from them just as you have. In this way, having wealth becomes meaningful. Lack of understanding and realization of impermanence causes us to be attached to our possessions. We must therefore practice to develop more satisfaction and generosity, and a more flexible way of caring.

Suffering of Worrying about Being Separated from Loved Ones

This kind of suffering (nyen dang dal dog kyi dhug ngal) is a consequence of attachment. You will always consider yourself to be a parent to your children, even when they become parents themselves. When they suffer from injuries or sickness, you will always do your best to give them relief and support. Sometimes when they are sick, you suffer more than you would if you yourself were sick. You always care more for them than for yourself, and you will make every sacrifice to give them the best life possible.

You will always suffer from the worry of not achieving your wishes. Without caring for yourself, you might even become involved in nonvirtuous actions in order to try to fulfill your loved ones' needs or

56

desires. You also generate kindness, love, and concern for all your loved ones, wishing for their health and happiness. Some people spend their whole life in this way. Even though your child, whom you care about more than yourself, may disappoint you, you still sacrifice yourself and continue to suffer on their behalf.

Suffering of a Lack of Basic Needs

This suffering (med pa tsal ne mi nyed pi dhug ngal) results from a lack of cultivation of merits and generosity. For instance, certain persons suffer from hunger or being without clothes or housing, and are forced to beg in the streets without encountering any compassion. When they see that someone else has perfect conditions in his life even if he does not deserve those conditions, they will still strongly desire that level of perfection. As with all beings, we also have a strong desire to live a happy life, be filled with joy, and have a nice family. Somehow, this does not always happen as we would wish. Instead, there is one thing that is more powerful than our wishes — our own karma. No matter what your wishes are, your karma will follow its own way. No matter what effort you make to fulfill your desires, you will fail and your hopes will remain just empty expectations. This causes you to suffer day and night.

Your whole life is full of desire. You desire delicious food but there may be no way to obtain it. You may have nothing to eat, no place to sleep at night, no treatment when sick, and no hope of any prayers or rituals when dying. Your dead body may be treated carelessly. This is the suffering of the lack of fulfilled desires.

In order to prevent a repetition of this suffering in your next life and to be relieved from it in your present life, it is important that you practice generosity. This does not mean giving away material offerings or objects. Rather, this refers to how mindful you are in your offering practice. You can cultivate great merits through the mental practice of generosity.

It is possible to make offerings purely in one's mind. These may be beautiful gardens, temples, or precious jewels. You can even mentally offer the whole universe purely from your heart to the Three Jewels: the enlightened ones (Sangye), the teachings (Bön), and the great spiritual masters who have the mind of the enlightened ones (Yungdrung Sempa). You can dedicate the benefits from this practice for all sentient beings.

Suffering of the Fear of Loss of One's Wealth

This suffering (yöd pa tso kyong mi tup pi dhug ngal), the complete opposite of the previous one, is caused by having more than you need, compounded by a lack of understanding regarding the practice of generosity. This means that although you are very wealthy, you are too greedy and too attached to give anything away. You are not ready to give mentally or spiritually, whether that involves spending money on yourself, giving it to help the needy, or supporting spiritual purposes.

It is important to know how to use your material goods and to be able to let go of them at the right time and for the right purpose. Otherwise, all you have is useless and will give you no satisfaction. You may even sacrifice your life for material possessions. In this way, neither this life nor the next one will be meaningful. When we have a perfect condition, we need to have a good understanding of the nature of impermanence, and hence understand that everything we own may be gone tomorrow.

There have been countries and people with rich cultures, but today nothing is left of them. Relying on material conditions is a mistake. This is also applicable to individuals. Instead of relying on material conditions to support you throughout your life, take advantage of having a perfect material condition, utilizing it for a good purpose while you have the chance. Dedicate this perfect situation to improving conditions for all sentient beings.

The purpose of giving examples of the eight different levels of suffering is not to give a specific number, but to show how limited we are by the qualities of this cyclic existence (khorwa). In order to overcome suffering, it is essential to reflect on each of the eight levels. You must realize the different types of suffering and reflect especially on the ones that are causing you the most difficulty. The purpose of this practice is not to alarm you, but to warn you and wake you up while there is still time to overcome suffering.

UNDERSTANDING THE LAW OF CAUSE AND RESULT

An essential part of the Bön teachings is to understand and realize the consequences of the law of cause and result (le gyu dre) in our day-to-day lives. Deeds of the body, mind, and speech, can have powerful results. As a practitioner, you will become more aware of how important and valuable the teachings on the law of cause and result are. These teachings will make a difference in both your present life and your rebirth.

The fruits of all your deeds, both positive and negative, will consequently manifest in your life and you will experience their effects.

They will ceaselessly accompany you throughout your life. This is comparable to a bird flying in the sky. No matter how high the bird flies, his shadow will follow him inseparably on the ground and will unite with him where he lands.

There is not a single result that appears without having a cause. The circumstances in our present life, whether pleasant or unpleasant, are a result of our actions. It is important to understand this law in a deeper sense in order to realize that it is necessary to practice virtuous deeds and avoid nonvirtuous deeds.

The Nonvirtuous Deeds

The nonvirtuous deeds (mi gewi le) are caused by the five poisons (dhug nga) and result in the ten nonvirtuous actions and their fruits. According to one of the *Dho* texts, in order to overcome nonvirtuous actions it is essential firstly to identify the poisons that cause them, and then to avoid them. Without purifying or overcoming the five poisons there is no way to achieve enlightenment. Just as a doctor has to diagnose the cause of an illness and then prescribe the proper medication in order to cure it, we have to realize how the five poisons affect us and then apply the antidote by practicing. Through this practice we will increase our awareness in order to slowly subdue the power of the five poisons, each of which is described below.

The Five Poisons

1. Ignorance (Timug)   Ignorance keeps us in complete darkness and dullness, not knowing or understanding the true nature of mind. We are unable to see the clear distinction between virtuous and nonvirtuous deeds, or to realize the power of the law of cause and result. Ignorance is very much like the monsoon season, during which things cannot be seen in their full beauty because of the mist.

2. Attachment (Döchag)   We need to be able to let go of our possessions and cease always wanting more and more. This desire for possessions has no end and no possibility of satisfaction. This is the suffering caused by being governed by the poison of attachment.

This is comparable to drinking salt water when you are thirsty. Your thirst will not be quenched and you will continue to suffer from the lack of water. Another example would be to see something that does not belong to you that you want very much, even though you know it is impossible to have it. This seething desire is very much like boiling water that keeps bubbling on the fire unless you turn the fire off.

It is essential to detach yourself from these material conditions and apply the practice of the nature of impermanence. You need to know how to let go of or utilize these objects in a better way. Who knows what life will bring next and how long these material goods will remain in your power?

All this happens because of a lack of understanding and satisfaction. We must understand how to be satisfied with and appreciate the conditions we live in as they are. Otherwise, we will never be satisfied. There is a saying in Tibet, "If we practice being happy the way we are now, then we will be satisfied and able to overcome attachment."

3. Anger (Zhedang)   Anger is the most powerful of the five poisons. The benefits of a lifetime of practice can be destroyed by only a minute of strong anger. In order to overcome anger, it is necessary always to be aware of and attentive to your inner thoughts.

Anger can arise when someone you dislike uses harsh language toward you. Immediately, your inner peace can be disturbed and you may respond with harsh words. You lose control of your body's actions, and the energy of the inner element of fire heats up as though blown by a high wind.

You must think carefully and be aware in order to overcome this poison. Instead of reacting in a negative way, try to understand that the anger within you is more dangerous and harmful to yourself than any external enemy. Control this inner enemy by applying the practice of love, kindness, and compassion for all sentient beings. This practice will also help you overcome any external enemies.

One of the great masters, Je Gur Shog Pa, was asked by one of his students, "Master, I turn angry very easily. Please teach me to help me better control my anger." The answer from the teacher was, "If you are looking at it like subduing an external enemy, that is too much. Better to think about taming and schooling your own thoughts. Then you will be able to control your anger."

4. Pride (Ngagyal)   Pride is defined as considering yourself as being better than others. It means imagining yourself to be in a higher position than others or better educated, or thinking that you possess more wealth or knowledge. You are always trying to make others look worse and lower than yourself. This attitude and behavior will hinder you from seeing the qualities of others and learning from them.

We must realize our interdependence. There is always something we can learn from those around us. It is necessary to begin living and thinking with genuine openness so that we can learn from others. There is always someone better informed or more powerful than you, or with other qualities that are not as strong in you. Others are worthy of your respect. Not being able to overcome your pride is very much like an iron ball that cannot absorb water, even though it is left out in the rain for years. Similarly, even though wise and well-read persons surround you, you have no way to receive their wisdom because your pride has completely blocked your entrance to their knowledge.

5. *Jealousy (Trakdog)* Jealousy can arise when you see that others are happy and lucky: they are living a better life, having a higher position, or possessing greater wealth than you. This shows that your own capacity to accept and enjoy another's good fortune and happiness is very narrow. Your lack of understanding of the vastness of your own inner capacity causes you to believe that good things happen only to others and never to yourself.

Imprisoned in your jealousy, you generate negative thoughts and actions in order to prevent good circumstances for others. You fear that another's success will result in a loss for you.

Therefore, it is crucial to concede that we ourselves would enjoy those same circumstances, and that others have the right to relish them as well. Everybody deserves luck and happiness. It is natural for human beings to long for better things. Through practice we can train our minds to be more flexible and open so that we can more easily accept good situations for ourselves and others.

For all sentient beings, and especially for us as practitioners, the most dangerous enemies are our own five poisons. If we do not free ourselves from these poisons, we cannot achieve enlightenment. However, any sentient being has the ability to overcome the five poisons.

You need to be attentive to every one of your actions so that you can correct your mistakes and make a commitment to not make them again. If you do not constantly draw your attention to these poisons, you will not be able to subdue them and you will gradually fall deeper and deeper under their influence. The precious life of this perfect human body will find its end without having fulfilled its purpose of achieving enlightenment and helping to free all sentient beings from the suffering of this cyclic world.

We can apply the teachings as an antidote to the poisons by practicing according to the Pathway of Renunciation of Dho (Pong Lam Dho), the Pathway of Transformation of Sang Ngag (Gyur Lam Ngag), or the Pathway of Self-Liberation or Dzogchen (Dol Lam Dzogpa Chenpo). It is important to choose whichever of these paths will be the most beneficial in your daily life and the most suitable according to your own level of awareness.

The ten nonvirtuous deeds are mainly caused by the influence of the five poisons. They are categorized by the three nonvirtuous deeds of the body (lü kyi mi gewa sum), the four nonvirtuous deeds of speech (ngag kyi mi gewa zhi), and the three nonvirtuous deeds of the mind (yid kyi mi gewa sum), each of which is described below.

The Three Nonvirtuous Deeds of the Body

1. Taking a Life (Sog Chodpa)   This can be generated by three of the five main poisons: anger, ignorance, and attachment. For instance, life can be taken during a war, which is mainly based on anger. We can also take life because of attachment, due to the wish to eat meat or to possess a fur coat. We can also take the life of another because of ignorance, or a lack of clear understanding of positive and negative cause and effect. We may believe that we are not involved in taking the lives of any beings, but in reality each and every person is involved in this nonvirtuous deed. Whether we are vegetarian or nonvegetarian, we eat by killing animals and plants. Even when walking on the ground we kill microscopic beings. For this reason we all need to purify ourselves continuously of these negative deeds.

2. Stealing (Ma Jin Lenpa)   This is the wish to obtain a material object, directly or indirectly, by force or robbery. Our intention is to possess something no matter what we must do to get it. Our attachment can lead us to commit this deed. It is most important to develop detachment from material objects in order to avoid the wish to steal.

3. Sexual Misconduct (Log Yem)   This concerns lay practitioners in particular because they take vows of abstinence on special days, such as the birthday of Tönpa Shenrab, birth and death anniversaries of other great masters, and full-moon days in monasteries. Having a sexual relationship without the consent of one's partner is also considered sexual misconduct.

The Four Nonvirtuous Deeds of Speech

1. Telling Lies (Zün Mawa)   This nonvirtuous deed has two aspects: telling lies with the intent to harm or mislead others and telling lies lightly without the intent to harm anybody. The most serious lie is to give another person the impression that you have wisdom or knowledge that you do not really possess. Telling your teacher that you see God, deities, or other visions, which in reality you have never seen, is a lie that has extremely negative results. It is common for human beings to try to gain a temporary benefit by lying without caring about the resulting negative effects. It is wiser to consider the long-term consequences for yourself and others before you make a decision to tell a lie, since lies can cause suffering. Lies, unlike truth, do not have the energy of everlasting strength.

2. Deliberately Causing Problems Between Friends (Tra Ma)   This nonvirtuous deed will occur when you generate negative thoughts toward friends or community based on jealousy and narrowness of thought. You destroy true closeness between persons when your intent is to tell lies in order to break up a friendship. This is a powerful negative act because you have injured the innocent hearts of genuine friends. You have planted the seeds of poison among them, which keep growing until the friends realize your deceitful intent. Even if they then purify their negative thoughts, you will not be free from receiving the negative results of this action because you were the source. We should be aware that our negative conduct will affect ourselves as well as others. You should instead cultivate positive merits and virtuous deeds that can result in happiness and joy, and bring together those separated by deliberate malice.

3. Harsh Language (Tsig Tsup) This nonvirtuous deed is one of the most powerful deeds that will harm you. There is a saying in Tibetan, "The harsh word has no weapon, but it will still cut your heart into pieces." Whenever we speak with someone, it is important to be aware of the words we are using. Harsh words are not necessarily spoken loudly or in anger. Words that are spoken politely may also cause harm to beings, even when the person involved is not present. Harsh language generates very energetic anger or jealousy, so we have to be careful how we talk to family, friends, elders, and others. Pointing out others' weaknesses in public is like putting a finger into their eye. In order to overcome this behavior, one has to learn how to speak properly with genuine, loving, and truthful intent.

4. Gossip (Ngag Khyal) This nonvirtuous deed can occur with or without intent. For example, we often spend our time with friends talking about things with no particular aim in mind. That is unintentional gossip. But there can also be gossip purposely created in order to put you into the limelight. Mainly, gossip means spending your time talking or laughing without any aim or goal. This activity is considered a waste of time.

The Three Nonvirtuous Deeds of the Mind

1. Negative Thoughts (Ngen Sem)   This nonvirtuous deed is the generation of negative thoughts. If you see an object that you would like to have, it may stay in your mind and your attraction to it may grow stronger. It holds your attention even if you do not possess it. Another example is if you see someone having a happy and successful life, you may generate evil thoughts that he or she should not experience joy or success.

2. Harmful Thoughts Toward Others (Nod Sem)   This nonvirtuous deed is similar to but more violent than negative thoughts (ngen sem). It means a willingness to consider harming or destroying others in order to cause misery. When you see others' joy and happiness, or see them living in luxury, and you raise harmful thoughts, such as wishing to destroy their happiness, hoping for bad things to happen to them, or directing harmful thoughts toward them, this is nod sem.

Wanting someone to lose something or, in a larger sense, thinking about killing someone is more apt to occur under the influence of anger. There are also aspects of jealousy involved in harmful thoughts toward others.

3. Wrong Views Toward the Teachings (Log Ta)   This nonvirtuous deed of the mind is a result of lack of understanding of the essential spiritual aspects of the teachings. Depending on one's karma, there are a variety of views that may manifest that could be called wrong, such as nonbelief in the truth of the law of cause and result, or nonbelief in past births and future rebirths. Other wrong views are not accepting that enlightenment can be achieved as result of practice, or not accepting the truth and quality of the Bön teaching. All of these support and follow the path of wrong views. As described in the text *Mutek Tsar Chö Ten Tsik Tek Dho,* there are 360 different types of wrong views, which can be simplified to 99 types of wrong views. In the simplest classification, there are two main nonbeliever traditions: eternalism (tag ta) and nihilism (che ta).

If you view the teachings as being insignificant or unimportant, you block yourself from entering the spiritual path and benefiting from its positive qualities. It is therefore important to trust, believe, and respect all aspects of the teachings in order to achieve a better human existence. The end of our life is death. All of us will experience the result of our own negative deeds and thoughts at that very last moment.

All of the negative deeds of our mind are aimed at intentionally harming others. All harmful thoughts toward others show a lack of understanding of love and compassion. Therefore, it is important to reflect on the essence of love and compassion in order to generate more positive thoughts toward others and life in general. This practice also helps us to develop openness and flexibility.

The law of cause and result is simply true. Every aspect of your virtuous deeds will result in peace, happiness, and goodness. In the same way, all nonvirtuous deeds of body, mind, and speech will cause you and others to experience suffering and unhappiness. The best course of action is to purify your negative deeds, develop your inner wisdom, and become involved in practice. To become liberated from nonvirtuous deeds, you need to practice generosity with pure intention. This is of benefit, even if it involves offering only a single flower or a stick of incense. You may also offer things mentally by manifesting them in your mind.

The Ten Virtuous Deeds

Practitioners must strictly practice the ten virtuous deeds (gewi le chu), which are:
1. avoiding the taking of another's life,
2. practicing generosity,
3. being mindful,
4. following moral discipline to overcome sexual misconduct,
5. telling the truth and avoiding telling lies,
6. trying to bring together friends who have separated (instead of separating friends by spreading rumors),
7. speaking peacefully and calmly instead of using harsh language,
8. being involved in practice (reciting prayers and recitations rather than wasting time on gossip),
9. being free from evil thoughts toward others (generating love and kindness rather than harmful thoughts toward others), and
10. being free from wrong views toward the teachings (realizing the truth of the law of cause and result, and entering the spiritual pathway).

The result of your virtuous and nonvirtuous deeds either forces you to take birth in this cyclic world of suffering or liberates you to achieve enlightenment.

Chapter 4

Nine Preliminary Practices

The student's mind needs to be prepared in order to take the first step into the practice, the nine preliminary practices (Ngöndro). After having opened your mind to receive the teachings, you have examined your motivation and gained some awareness of the five poisons and their pervasive influence. You have contemplated the rareness of the perfect human body and its nature of impermanence, and the suffering of this cyclic existence. You have increased your awareness of the law of cause and result. You are now ready to begin Ngöndro.

Each of the following nine preliminary practices will help you to understand more deeply the qualities of the practice and how to apply them to your day-to-day life. These methods will help you to gain stability and confidence in the practice. The six practices and the three recitations that comprise the nine preliminary practices are as follows.

- *Generating the Mind of Enlightenment (Thegchen Semkyed)* is also described as the door to the pathway of the greater vehicles.
- *Taking Refuge (Kyabdro)* is surrendering yourself to the Three Jewels: the enlightened ones (Sangye), the teachings of Tönpa

Shenrab (Bön), and the great masters who have achieved the mind of the enlightened ones (Yungdrung Sempa). You are thus seeking protection from the suffering of this cyclic world as well as blessings and strength to achieve the ultimate goal of practice.

- *Confession (Shagpa)* of nonvirtuous activities is practiced in order to purify nonvirtuous deeds and their negative karmas.
- *Mandala Offering (Mandal Bulwa)* is the practice of offering mandalas in order to cultivate good merit and receive blessings from the enlightened ones.
- *Connecting with the Teacher (Lamai Naljor)* is the practice whereby the student seeks blessings from his or her root teacher in order to realize the true natural state of mind.
- *Prostrations (Chak)* involve using one's body, mind, and speech together to purify the negative deeds of the three doors.

In addition, the following Three Essential Recitations of Bön (Nyingpo Nam Sum) are practiced:

- SA LE ÖD, the recitation of the Buddha of Compassion;
- MA TRI, the recitation of Tönpa Shenrab and the loving mother Chamma, which is done in order to connect with and seek blessings from the six liberators of the six realms;
- DHU TRI SU, the recitation of purification.

According to the advice of Shardza Tashi Gyaltsen, one should complete the first six practices sequentially: generating the mind of enlightenment (semkyed), taking refuge (kyabdro), confession (shagpa),

72

performing the mandala offering (mandal bulwa), connecting with the teacher (lamai naljor), and prostrations (chak). The three essential recitations (nyingpo nam sum) are practiced either separately or with the prostrations. It is important to complete each practice 100,000 times. Completing this practice depends very much on one's time and favorable conditions. Ngöndro can be practiced gradually in steps or all together, as you are able. Correctly translated prayers will be effective in any language. In any event, you should be sure to complete all the preliminary practices and all the required accumulations. If you are not able to fulfill them all at once, do as much as you can in each session, always having very pure intention.

If you want to complete all of the practices at one retreat, then do 1,000 semkyed, 1,000 kyabdro, 1,000 shagpa, 1,000 mandal bulwa, 1,000 lamai naljor, and 1,000 chak with the nyingpo nam sum recitations each day. In this way, you will be able to complete all the preliminary practices in one hundred days.

Whichever way you do the preliminary practices, it is important to complete and have a good understanding of the practices of generating the mind of enlightenment and taking refuge, as well as the dedication prayer, even in one session. By completing each of these recitations and practices 100,000 times, you will have completed all of the 900,000 accumulations of the preliminary practices.

PRELIMINARY PRACTICE 1: GENERATING THE MIND OF ENLIGHTENMENT

The ultimate goal of the practice is to achieve enlightenment and be liberated completely from the suffering of this cyclic world. It is important to understand the sources of suffering of all sentient beings and know the ways to overcome them. This is in accordance with the view of the greater vehicles: to generate the mind of enlightenment (thegchen semkyed) on the basis of love and compassion and develop this mind of enlightenment in order to benefit all sentient beings.

At first, this means that you have to be conscious of the fact that any relationship between yourself and every other sentient being is like the bond between a mother and her child. You may face difficulties generating this attitude at the beginning, but if you explore this more deeply and try to understand it, then naturally you can generate compassion toward any being. We often do not realize the nature of our relationships, but it is certain that in one way or another, in countless lifetimes from the beginning until now, we have been circulating in this cyclic world, bound in relationship to all beings.

For example, if we fry a whole pot of black corn with only one grain of white corn and mix them together, the single white kernel will eventually touch each and every one of the black kernels, although it may be hard to tell which one of the black kernels has already touched the white one. We can know with certainty that at some point each black kernel will have been touched by the white one. This is very similar to the way we are in relationship to all other sentient beings. In the relationship with your present mother you have probably experienced great love and care for each other each and every moment. All the sentient beings who at one time have been your mother have given you the same love and care, even though you may view them in this present life as enemies. If you focus only on the physical level of what you feel and experience about someone, then you may not realize the nature of the energetic love and compassion shown to you by that sentient being in the past. There is nothing that solidly or independently remains of these thoughts and feelings. Whether someone is considered to be an enemy or a friend, all is changing according to circumstances and conditions. Therefore, there are meaningful reasons to generate love and compassion toward all sentient beings, and wish to liberate them all from the suffering of this cyclic world. It is your responsibility to care for them as a son or daughter, and generate the mind of enlightenment from the deep core of your heart.

Make a commitment to dedicate from this moment on each and every aspect of your practice to all sentient beings without any concept or view of them as an enemy or a close friend. Since all thoughts of partiality or dislike will hinder you from fully realizing the practice, you must free yourself from these conceptual thoughts.

To do this, generate unconditional love and compassion for each and every being without condition. Try to focus on a particular person whom you feel uncomfortable with and consider as an enemy. As you think of this person, try to decrease the power of anger and hatred toward them, and increase your compassion and love toward them as those of a mother toward a child. Practice in this way until you feel that it is easy to generate love and compassion toward them.

In order to be able to generate the mind of enlightenment toward all sentient beings, the key is to create a good foundation by practicing the Four Immeasurables (Tsemed Zhi):

- limitless compassion (nyingje tsemed),
- limitless kindness (champa tsemed),

- limitless love (gawa tsemed), and
- limitless equanimity (tangnyom tsemed).

These four are interrelated and complement each other.

This practice starts with the last one. Firstly, we practice to always feel limitless equanimity toward all sentient beings and then we practice to generate love equally to all sentient beings. After that, we practice to treat all sentient beings with equal love and kindness. Finally, we practice to generate limitless compassion for all sentient beings. Without understanding equanimity toward all sentient beings, we will not be able to generate love for those we do not know or those we hate and consider as enemies.

It is most important to overcome the conception of partiality, which means that you differentiate your attitude among sentient beings according to the circumstances. Make an effort to understand and reflect on the positive aspects of the love and compassion that others have given you in the past, rather than thinking about the negative aspects that make you angry or cause you to hate them. Once you are able to realize the equality among all sentient beings, you will be better able to generate love toward all of them. Having a sense of love for all sentient beings automatically generates care and support for them with kindness.

When you have perfected these three levels, compassion will manifest more easily and actively, and then the mind of enlightenment will be realized naturally. Without having limitless compassion toward sentient beings, you will not be able to manifest any actions of body, mind, and speech that can be helpful to others.

The partial attitude of compassion that we all have does not help all sentient beings. Pure compassion must be generated for those who are most needful, most weak in their abilities and conditions, and most dependent on others. Then you can manifest complete devotion in a practical way to help them, instead of just wishing or thinking or meditating about compassion. The meditation on the practice of compassion is only to prepare you to be active in a practical way as needed. When this attitude grows and develops more and more powerfully, it will lead to the transformation of achieving the mind of enlightenment.

The mind of enlightenment can be categorized in three different levels according to your realization or knowledge. Examples provided in the text *Kun Tu Le* are: the attitudes of a shepherd, a tour guide, and a skipper. The shepherd's main purpose is to take care of his animals by looking for a good place (where there is no risk of wild animals) for them to find grass and water, and making sure that all of his animals are protected before he cares for himself. This is like wanting to liberate all sentient beings from suffering before achieving one's own liberation. The tour guide first visits and learns about a particular place before he brings tourists along to show them that place and be their guide. This is like wanting to liberate oneself and achieve enlightenment first, and then liberate all other sentient beings. The skipper reaches the shore simultaneously with all his passengers. This is like wanting to reach enlightenment and liberate all sentient beings at the same time as oneself.

The highest level is the way of the shepherd because in this case one is thinking about others first. The attitude of the tour guide is the lowest level because one is thinking firstly about oneself and about the others only afterwards. The attitude of the skipper is the middle level because his way of thinking is to liberate all sentient beings at the same time.

The mind of enlightenment can also be categorized in two levels according to two essential aspects: the absolute mind of enlightenment and the relative mind of enlightenment. You will only be able to generate the absolute mind of enlightenment once you have achieved the realization of the natural state of mind. The relative mind of enlightenment has two aspects: one is a more wishful mind of enlightenment and the other is a more active mind of enlightenment. The second one is more actively involved in practicing to liberate all sentient beings.

Whichever practice we are discussing, the aim of all of them is to achieve the enlightenment of all sentient beings. To accomplish this, we have to practice generosity, moral discipline, patience or tolerance, enthusiasm, and contemplation, and in this way achieve realizations. While increasing our energy and good qualities for the benefit of other sentient beings, we can also practice enthusiastically generating the mind of enlightenment during all our activities.

How to Meditate on Generating the Mind of Enlightenment

Meditation Posture

In order to practice properly, it is important to sit in the proper meditation posture. Sit cross-legged on the floor, resting your hands palms-up on your lap and pressing your thumbs at the base of your ring fingers. Straighten your spine and keep your neck in a normal upright position without bending it too much, open your shoulders, close your eyes, and leave your mouth open slightly.

Visualization

Visualize in the space above your crown wheel (or chakra) a golden throne lifted up by snow lions. On that throne is a lotus throne with sun and moon cushions. Visualize Shen Lha Ökar, the Buddha of Compassion, as inseparable from the real form of your root teacher. See his body clearly as white in color and wearing his full ornaments.

Imagine that Shen Lha Ökar is facing you. All the master lineage holders appear just above his crown wheel, extending upwards to Kuntu Zangpo, the Primordial Enlightened One, like a string of golden prayer beads.

On Shen Lha Ökar's right side are flames of fire and gusts of wind. The retinue of peaceful and wrathful deities stands in these flames and gusts. They wear ornaments made of bone. Each deity holds weapons. They stand in wrathful postures. Above and behind these deities are the 1,002 enlightened ones, dressed in monks' robes. They are all perfected with the thirty-two major signs of the enlightened ones and eighty-one exemplary signs. They all sit cross-legged in the meditation position. They emanate limitless lights and rays and are surrounded by circular rainbows.

To the left of Shen Lha Ökar, in the center of a rainbow, stand all of the khadros. They are of different colors, and all are wearing ornaments of bone and standing in the dancing position. The chief of the khadros, Kalpa Sangmo, is surrounded by the khadros of the four castes and the khadros of the three times.

Above and behind them is Tönpa Shenrab, surrounded by his eight great sons and the great masters of the Three Vehicles. Their bodies are white and they are dressed in monks' robes. Each holds a staff topped with a stupa (kharsil) in the right hand and a begging bowl (lhungze) in the left hand. They are standing one above the other, though without touching.

Behind Shen Lha Ökar is the throne of the everlasting Yungdrung. Positioned on that throne are the Three Supreme Objects, which symbolize the body, mind, and speech of the enlightened ones. A statue and a thangka, which are as huge as a mountain, symbolize the body. All the texts of the teachings, wrapped in cloths with their labels facing toward you, are making the sounds "ali" and "kali"; they symbolize the speech. There are 1,002 stupas, which are as bright as light reflected off a snow-covered mountain, that symbolize the mind. Above and behind these is Yum Chenmo Satrik Ersang, who is Sherab Chamma, the great wisdom mother. She is the chief of the Twenty-One Loving Mothers (Chamma Nyer Chig). She wears the thirteen peaceful ornaments and is surrounded by her retinues.

Then, below and in front of Shen Lha Ökar, in the space of flames and wind, is Yeshe Walmo, the chief protector of the Bön teachings. The other protectors of the Bön teachings surround her. All of them face backwards, representing the renunciation of all the obstacles to the practices. Bear in mind that all of these protectors are here to protect and support you in your practice.

This visualization also applies to the other preliminary practices described below.

It is important to know that all of these deities and objects are like a shining star in the sky, or a cloud appearing in space. All of them are colorful and bright. They are all present for the benefit of sentient beings, with their compassion and wisdom, with their watchful eyes and listening ears, and with their presence. Know that all sentient beings have been your mother, and you have been wandering in this cyclic world for a long time. You have been born in the upper and lower realms, in different forms. All of the sentient beings raised you with kindness and love when they were your parents. Their help and support is limitless. All of these beings who have been your parents and who are so kind, are in the prison of suffering. Their wisdom is obscured by thick clouds of ignorance. They are unable to distinguish the path of enlightenment from the nonpath. They are far away from qualified teachers who can guide them on the true path of enlightenment. They wander in the cyclic world like a helpless blind person roaming in the street. You have the responsibility of taking care of these parent beings, because you owe them for their kindness and enlightened qualities. You must practice the mind of enlightenment on behalf of all sentient beings. You are following in the path of the spiritual masters of the past who performed great deeds. You must achieve enlightenment in this lifetime and be a great liberator of sentient beings. Ask for the blessing, guidance, and protection of the union of the Four Supreme Objects — the Lama and the Three Jewels — so that you may accomplish your goal to liberate all sentient beings.

Recitation

When you are doing the practice of generating the mind of enlightenment in order to complete your accumulations of this part of the preliminary practices, recite the short form of the following prayer:

Ji tar gyal wa phak pa ji zhin du
Di sok due sum ge we ghu pal gyi
Sem chen sang gye thop par ja we chir
Dak ni jang chup chok tu sem kyed do

As do the enlightened ones and the spiritual warriors,
By the blessings and power of these virtuous deeds of the three times,
To attain enlightenment for all sentient beings
I generate the mind of enlightenment.

This prayer needs to be recited 100,000 times. When you recite it, you generate the mind of enlightenment in the same way that spiritual masters have done in the past. Dedicate all your virtuous deeds throughout the limitless past until now, those that you are doing at the present time, and those that you will continue to do in the future until you attain enlightenment, for the benefit of all sentient beings.

By doing this practice, you are generating the precious mind of enlightenment, which will allow you to accomplish the goals of achieving enlightenment and manifesting as a great liberator of sentient beings. By doing this, and by the blessings, powers, and qualities of the root virtues of the three times, you will carry all sentient beings, from the top level of the cyclic world to the bottom of the hell realm, without exception, across the ocean of suffering to reach enlightenment.

Contemplation

When you are ending your session, dissolve all sentient beings in the form of rays of light into the space where you have visualized the enlightened ones. Then, dissolve all of those visions into the central figure of Shen Lha Ökar, which then dissolves into light that flows into you. Think that you have received the quality of the absolute mind of enlightenment and meditate without the distraction of thoughts.

Dedication

When you finish your meditation on generating the mind of enlightenment, it is essential that you dedicate all the merit you have generated to all sentient beings with the aspiration that they be liberated from this cyclic world by reciting the following dedication prayer:

Go sum dag pi ge wa gang gi pa
Kham sum sem chen nam gyi don du ngo
Dü sum sag pi le dip kun jang ne
Ku sum zog pi sang gye nyur top shog

All virtuous deeds of the three doors of my body, mind, and speech
I dedicate for the benefit of all sentient beings of the three realms.
By purifying all the negative actions and obscurations accumulated
  in the three times,
May all sentient beings swiftly achieve enlightenment.

It is very important to repeat the practice of Thegchen Semkyed regularly until you have an inner sense of genuine realization, rather than just a conceptual understanding of the importance of the mind of enlightenment. Once you have achieved this realization, your whole wisdom, attitude, and character will be completely transformed. Every one of your deeds or words will be more meaningful to others.

The practice of generating the mind of enlightenment is like the most precious jewel. It is the essence of all the teachings of Bön, the root of the pathway to achieving enlightenment and realizing the true quality of the sources of enlightenment. Without entering this pathway, there is no way of achieving enlightenment. Therefore, we all must value this practice and utilize it in a positive way. This is the first step of entering into the four pathways of training:

- the path of accumulation (tsog lam),
- the path of action (jor lam),
- the path of seeing (thong lam), and
- the path of meditation (gom lam).

Together these open the fifth pathway, which is the path beyond training (mi lop lam).

PRELIMINARY PRACTICE 2:
TAKING REFUGE

The purpose of taking refuge (kyabdro) in the Three Jewels is to receive blessings and be protected from the suffering of this cyclic existence. In order to seek refuge you have to realize truly the suffering of this cyclic existence. Refuge also depends on your trust and faith in the Three Jewels. Accordingly, you will receive protection and blessings from them. Trust is the key to opening the door to Bön and its wisdom. This practice in particular has to be based especially on trust and faith.

According to Dzogchen texts, trust can be divided into four categories:

- Trust of Inspiration,
- Trust of Clarity,
- Trust of Trust, and
- Trust of Accomplishment.

Trust of inspiration can be generated by visiting holy places and by meeting great masters and seeing their way of living and behaving. This makes you follow them the way a child follows his or her mother with joy and happiness. This trust is mainly generated by the inspiring examples of great masters and teachers. We are inspired to be close to our teachers and other practitioners, and follow the instructions of the teachings. At the same time, it is necessary to look within, and contemplate and understand the rareness of the perfect human body and the uncertainty of remaining in this state. Due to impermanence, you can be born in any of the realms, and it is quite certain that you will experience suffering according to conditions there. Trust of inspiration also arises from either seeing the condition of others who are involved seriously in the practice, cultivating great merits, and enjoying the very positive results of the practice, or by seeing those who cultivate negative actions which cause them to suffer. Therefore, be aware of yourself and follow the right pathway of practice.

Trust of clarity means that you have a clear understanding of how to distinguish between the quality of suffering of this cyclic existence and the purity and joy of the enlightened ones. At the same time, you are fully aware of the causes of these two qualities and you know which to avoid and which to absorb. This is very much like a filter that you throw into a fountain full of cloudy water that will clear the water immediately.

Trust of trust is mainly generated by inspiration and your own belief (with clear understanding and without any doubt) that the ten nonvirtuous deeds are the main source of suffering in this cyclic existence and the ten virtuous deeds are the source of joy and happiness. You then apply this trust to your practice like stable ice that covers a lake in the middle of winter with no risk of breaking.

Trust of accomplishment helps you to continue the practice without distraction or interference. Whatever realizations you have achieved through the prior levels of trust, try to keep them stable without any change until you achieve the ultimate goal of your practice. Similarly, once you have died, you will not be able to change your mind and come back again in the same body. Trust of accomplishment can be achieved as the goal of practice as long as you have a stable understanding of the abovementioned trusts. Gradually, you will receive the blessings and powers of the Three Jewels and eventually you will realize the true natural state of mind, thus achieving the ultimate goal of being completely free from the suffering of this world forever, which is enlightenment.

Trust is not the only important quality in this particular practice. The main points are to develop your inner wisdom and realizations, to receive teachings and blessings from your teacher, and to receive blessings from the deities and protectors. This all depends on how much your realization of trust has grown. The blessings and power of wisdom do not depend on a physical aspect that becomes part of you, but rather on whether you are ready to receive those qualities by opening the door of your trust to them. This is like the example of the ring and the hook: the ring is your trust and the hook is the blessings of your teacher. When you are seeking your teacher's blessings, power, and protection purely from your heart, then regardless of distance and material conditions, the blessings are there as long as you are completely open to receive them without any doubt. When the two conditions — the blessings of your teacher and the openness of your heart — exist together, there is a way to connect the hook onto the ring. For this reason, it is essential to be always devoted to the Three Jewels and the teachings without any question or doubt.

How to Meditate on Refuge

Meditation Posture

When meditating on taking refuge (kyabdro), it is important to sit in the proper meditation posture (see full description in the beginning of "How to Meditate on Generating the Mind of Enlightenment" on pages 78–79).

Visualization

Transform the place where you are from its ordinary aspect, for example, the rocks and stones of a cave, into a beautiful and colorful land of pure gold decorated with turquoise. The ground is spongy, not hard, with uplifting flexibility. Surrounded by great auspicious trees, there is a river of nectar and there are seven precious objects, eight auspicious symbols, and other beautiful materials and surroundings. In the center of the sky are white clouds, like a huge cushion.

On this cushion of clouds is a jeweled throne with sun and moon cushions. On the sun and moon cushions is seated your root lama, who embodies all the qualities of all the enlightened beings of the three times, such as compassion, wisdom, and love. Your root lama is in the form of the Enlightened One of Compassion, Shen Lha Ökar, and is facing you with all the lineage holders just above his crown wheel, extending upwards like a string of golden prayer beads to the Primordial Enlightened One, Kuntu Zangpo. Continue the visualization as given on pages 79–80 for the first preliminary practice.

All your visualizations — the four supreme objects of refuge, the deities, the khadros, and the protectors — are clear and distinct but do not have material form, like an image in a mirror. So they exist but cannot be grasped, like the reflection of the moon on water. They all appear at the same time, yet they are separate, just as a rainbow is made up of separate colors. All are smiling happily in bright and colorful manifestations. Bear in mind that all appear with the perfect qualities of compassion, power, blessings, and omniscient knowledge.

Now imagine that all sentient beings on the earth are in front of the supreme objects of refuge. Visualize the person you consider your enemy, as well as the low-level beings that cause sickness, problems, or other obstacles, in front of you. To your right side, visualize your father of this lifetime. On your left, visualize your mother of this lifetime. Then visualize all sentient beings of the six realms gathered around you in the form of human beings at a festival. They hold their hands, palms together, in front of their hearts.

Think that for all sentient beings, including yourself, from today until we achieve enlightenment, the Lama (the teacher) and the Three

Jewels are the ones in whom we take refuge, whom we consider as our supporters. Think as if to say to them, "We rely on you; we have no one other than you in whom we can take refuge. So, the pleasure or suffering of our lives, and the guiding of our future path to enlightenment, these we entrust to you, our true protectors. Whether we are liberated or remain in this cyclic world is up to you in your wisdom."

Create this visualization from within as if you are really doing these actions.

Recitation

As you are counting accumulations of each preliminary practice as indicated above, do not separate the visualization you have generated from the prayer you are reciting. Reenergize your thoughts of taking refuge and recite the following prayer:

Shen rab la ma ku sum jung ne pal
Dü sum der shek dro wa yon kyi gön
Ku zug shal kyin du dung sung rab ten
Chog chü she rab thar lam tön pi don
Ne zhir chak tsal dro kun kyab su chi

The supreme teacher is the source of the three bodies of enlightenment,
All enlightened ones of the three times are the liberators of sentient beings,
These three symbols of body, mind, and speech are the reliable source
   of blessings of the enlightened ones,
The Great Spiritual Warriors of the Ten Directions are the lamps on
   the path of enlightenment,

All beings prostrate and take refuge in the Four Supreme Objects of Refuge.

As you recite this prayer, it is crucial to be aware and mindful of its meaning.

Contemplation

The light rays from the heart of the four supreme objects of refuge are reflected to all sentient beings, thereby purifying all impure deeds, obstacles, and negative karmic traces. Then all the sentient beings are dissolved into the four supreme objects at once, just as one hundred birds all fly if a pebble is thrown at one of them. Gradually all of the four supreme objects are transformed into light and dissolve into the central lama. The experiential lineage holders above the crown wheel of the lama dissolve into the lama, beginning with the highest one and continuing to the lowest. Then the lama's body grows smaller and smaller and moves to your crown wheel. You unify the lama's mind and your own mind into one mind. Imagine that your mind, by this unification, possesses the same threefold mind of wisdom as that of the lama. Its essence is the contemplation of that state of mind without modifying your mind, but relaxing in its own state without grasping and without being deluded. In reality, that is the absolute perfected precious mind and the ultimate object of refuge.

Dedication

When you finish each session of the practice of taking refuge, dedicate whatever merit you have obtained from these virtuous deeds to all sentient beings, so that they may obtain enlightenment, just as the great spiritual warriors of the past have done. In this way, recite the dedication prayer as given on page 83 for the first preliminary practice.

PRELIMINARY PRACTICE 3: CONFESSION

The purpose of the practice of confession (shagpa) is to purify the negative deeds that you have cultivated in the past, present, and future, not just the ones from this lifetime. We sentient beings are continuing to be reborn, life after life, in this cyclic world. During all this time, with and without intention, we have cultivated limitless nonvirtuous deeds. Their negative energy will continue to grow and obstruct us from developing our practice and realization unless we purify them. No matter how long ago or recent the cause of these nonvirtuous deeds, the continuity of their manifestation is there. The truth of the law of cause and result is always present. As long as a cause exists energetically, according to the time and conditions, the result of it will occur. This means that no matter what has been cultivated, its effect will be experienced.

To purify yourself from negative deeds, it is essential to accomplish the four powers of the practice of confession:

- the power of the witness,
- the power of regret,
- the power of commitment, and
- the power of the antidote.

The Power of the Witness

Meditate, if possible, in front of a statue of Tönpa Shenrab or an image of an enlightened deity or your teacher. If this is not possible, then visualize any of them above your crown wheel, with a complete awareness and feeling of their presence in front of you. Think about your nonvirtuous deeds of the past and present, especially the ones from the present that you regret. From the core of your heart, feel sorry about them and experience your regret. Ask sincerely to be accepted and blessed in order to purify those karmic traces that you are responsible for, and to be given the strength to practice and liberate all sentient beings.

The Power of Regret

Experience regret deeply from the heart and with all your thoughts, and feel sorry for all the nonvirtuous deeds that you may have done by the three doors of body, mind, and speech in the past, present, and future.

The Power of Commitment

In addition to the power of regret, it is important that you commit to doing certain practices, such as recitations and prayers. You must also commit to not repeating similar nonvirtuous deeds again.

The Power of the Antidote

The antidote is engaging in practice and reciting prayers in order to purify your deeds from the past, which will also help you keep your commitment not to become involved in the same nonvirtuous deeds again.

Once you have accomplished these four powers, you have discontinued the fruition of the negative results of your past deeds. This is as though you have eliminated the potential of seeds by frying or boiling them. For example, when you boil corn, its shape will not have changed but the potential for it to grow fruit is taken away. Likewise, you should clear all your negative deeds of body, mind, and speech. Even if you do not remember them all, consider all of them and include them all in your practice.

There are certain meditation and visualization methods that you should do when practicing confession as an antidote to purify the negativity of your deeds, and when you recite prayers.

How to Meditate on Confession

Meditation Posture

When meditating on confession (shagpa), it is important to sit in the proper meditation posture (see full description in the beginning of "How to Meditate on Generating the Mind of Enlightenment" on page 78–79).

Visualization

Visualize yourself as an ordinary being. Above your crown wheel, on a sun and moon cushion in the center of a thousand-petaled white lotus, imagine a bright SO syllable from which eight colorful rays of light are emanating and going upwards into space. These rays invite countless SO syllables from space, which have the quality of the compassionate ones who reside in space, and these dissolve into the original SO syllable. That SO syllable becomes much brighter and more glorious than before. Again, imagine rays of light emanating from the same SO syllable, straightforwardly cleansing all the pollution of the existing world and purifying the defilements of all sentient beings. Dissolve that SO syllable into light.

In reality, this SO syllable is your root teacher, who is the collective compassion of the enlightened ones of the three times, but appears in the form of Shen Lha Ökar, the compassionate one. His body color is clear and shining like thousands of sunbeams reflected off a snow-covered mountain. He has one face and two hands, and he is seated cross-legged. His two hands are in the gesture of meditation and hold a jeweled vase, full of nectar with the nine qualities of perfection and decorated with the thirteen peaceful ornaments. He appears in this form but is not a material object. Imagine that he is facing you, full of compassion and love for all sentient beings.

In front of him, you think very clearly from your heart about whatever nonvirtuous deeds you have done through the three doors of your body, mind, and speech, such as the five limitless nonvirtuous deeds, eight wrong deeds, nine deluded deeds, and so on, from the very beginning until now, in limitless lifetimes. Say, "I confess these nonvirtuous deeds, keeping none secret, hiding none. I regret these deeds, realize that they are wrong, and confess with the four conditions of confession. Please accept my confession and purify all the negative karmas and defilements, without exception, and protect me, kindly and lovingly."

Then, in the center of the moon disk at the heart of Shen Lha

Ökar, imagine that one hundred syllables (see below) are circulating counterclockwise around the SO syllable, as if forming a white rosary of syllables around the SO syllable. Focus on the circulating syllables and imagine you are reciting them. From those syllables, limitless light rays spontaneously begin to descend, in the form of the white nectar of wisdom mind. Shen Lha Ökar's body is filled with the nectar that showers down on him, and it overflows out of his crown wheel into the vase he holds. From that vase, the nectar overflows, showers down on your crown wheel, and fills your body. Because of this, all your sickness, obstacles, negative karma, and defilements are forced out of your body, through the pores of your skin, in the form of a reddish-blue liquid. This liquid flows under your cushion, down to the underworld, into the mouths of the Lord of Death and his retinue, to whom you owe karmic debts. Imagine that they are satisfied with your offering of the black liquid and your dedication of merit.

Recitation

Next, recite the hundred-syllable prayer as many times as you can:

> *So Mu Ye Tro Khyung Ye Lam Tri Tri Tar Dar Sal War Od Pag Ram*
> *So Ha*
> *So Mu Ra Ta Han Wer Ni Drum Hrun Mu Tre Mu Tre Mu Ra Mu Tre*
> *Mu Ye Mu Ye Ha Ra Mu Ye*
> *Mu Tro Mu Tro We Ro Mu Tro*
> *Mu Ni Gyer To Ye Khyab Khar Ro*
> *Tro Dal Hri Hro Wer Ni Wer Lo*
> *Shu La Wer Ro Na Hu Ta Ka*
> *Shu Dho Shu Dho Du Shu Dho Ya*

Sa Le Sa Le Tri Sa Le Ya
Sang Nge Sang Nge Su Sang Nge Ya
Mu Ra Ta Han Tri Tse Drung Mu
Ha Ha Drum Drum Ho Ho Lam Lam Hung Hung Phet Phet

Do as many repetitions of the hundred-syllable prayer as possible. By reciting the prayer and transmitting the black liquid to the Lord of Death and his retinue, they are satisfied and your karmic debts are paid. Imagine that all sentient beings are freed from negative karmic traces and sicknesses, and that your body is completely purified from all nonvirtuous deeds and becomes as clear as crystal, filled with the white nectar of the five wisdoms. From all 740,000 pores of your body, you shower all sentient beings with this nectar. By so doing, all nonvirtuous deeds and karmic traces are washed away and the external world is transformed into a pure spiritual land. Imagine that all sentient beings are transformed into the form of Shen Lha Ökar, all of them reciting the hundred-syllable prayer strongly. Then recite the hundred-syllable prayer and in this way complete 100,000 repetitions.

Contemplation

To conclude the session, imagine that all the manifestations of Shen Lha Ökar of the external world dissolve into light and dissolve into the Shen Lha Ökar that is above your crown. Imagine that the central Shen Lha Ökar appreciates that you are purified from your nonvirtuous deeds and defilements, and smiles. He dissolves into light, which is the unification of emptiness and bliss. This light then dissolves into you. Then rest in contemplation, seeing the face of the spontaneously arising Shen Lha Ökar, which is the true state of your mind.

Dedication

When you finish your meditation on confession, it is essential that you dedicate all the merit generated by your virtuous deeds for the liberation of all sentient beings from this cyclic world. Recite the dedication prayer as given on page 83 for the first preliminary practice.

PRELIMINARY PRACTICE 4:
MANDALA OFFERING

The purpose of cultivating merit by offering a mandala (mandal bulwa) is to make yourself more spacious and open, and thus be able to absorb and digest the valuable teachings without any obstacles to your practice. We human beings in our temporary state with this physical body depend on many circumstances — especially our good fortune — to receive the teachings, which is not something that is common to all. This only occurs based on the great efforts of your good merit in the past. It is still important to cultivate more merits in order to fulfill the goal of practice, especially two important merits: the causal merits of fortune (gyu sonam gyi tsog), which is compassion, and the fruition merits of wisdom (dewe yeshe kyi tsog), which is the wisdom to realize the true nature of mind.

The mandala itself symbolizes the universe. If you cannot offer a material mandala as an object, then you can offer a mandala with hand gestures (chag gya). The most important thing is to generate the pure attitude of offering to the Three Jewels with the purpose not of temporary material gain but rather deeper understanding in order to achieve the realization of your true state of mind, develop compassion for all sentient beings, and develop perfect strength and energy to follow the spiritual pathway until you achieve enlightenment.

If you are very mindful in this practice on a daily basis, you can manifest all these offerings mentally through visualization. For example, if you travel on the highway by night, all the streetlights of the cities and all the headlights of the cars can be transformed into butter lamps and you can make an offering of them to the Three Jewels with pure motivation. That is to say, the essence of offering the mandala is not the material object, but rather your own mindfulness and intention and being able to let go without attachment are the true offerings.

It is also of the highest importance not to feel regret or attachment toward the object once you have offered it. The more you do the mandala offering practice, the more you will experience the blessings of this teaching and develop your inner wisdom while doing your practice.

In order to cultivate good merit, you can also perform the practice of generosity, such as working on teaching texts to be published, contributing a few days or even only a few hours in the construction of a temple or stupa, and so forth.

How to Practice Mandala Offering

Meditation Posture

As with the other preliminary practices, for the mandala offering practice, always sit in the proper meditation posture (see full description in the beginning of "How to Meditate on Generating the Mind of Enlightenment" on pages 78–79).

Visualizations and Recitations

As in the visualization for the practice of taking refuge, you transform the ordinary place where you are into a beautiful land with great auspicious trees, a river of nectar, seven precious objects, eight auspicious symbols, and so forth. Visualize your root lama seated on a jeweled throne with sun and moon cushions in the form of Shen Lha Ökar, the Enlightened One of Compassion, along with all the supreme objects of refuge, exactly as described on pages 79–80 for the first preliminary practice.

If you are using a mandala plate, hold it in your left hand. Clean it with the heel of the right hand. Wipe the mandala plate three times counterclockwise, three times clockwise, and three times straight away from yourself. While doing so, imagine that you are cleaning the negative karmic traces and defilements of the universe. Recite the prayer of cleansing the impurities:

> *Bön nyid ye ne nam par dag pa zhin*
> *Sem nyid de zhin nam par dag pa te*
> *Bag chag dig pa ma lü sal we chir*
> *Sal we mandal yong su chi war ja wo*
> *Na Ma A Kar Sha Ya Ni Shag Sa Le Sang Nge Ye So Ha Chod Phur*
>   *Sa Le Ha Lo Sang*

> *As pure as the nature of Bön from the beginning,*
> *So is the nature of mind completely pure as it is.*
> *To clean all the karmic traces and defilements*
> *Thoroughly clean the perfect mandala.*
> *Na Ma A Kar Sha Ya Ni Shag Sa Le Sang Nge Ye So Ha*
>   *Chod Phur Sa Le Ha Lo Sang*

Still holding the mandala in the left hand, pick up the mandala offerings you have prepared with your right hand, such as flowers, rice, barley, corn, and so on. Make a boundary around the edge of the base of the mandala with your right hand and imagine that it is an open expanse of golden earth.

Then pick up the mandala offerings in your right hand again and place a handful in the center of the mandala, saying, "Drum Ri Ti Gar Ma La Ho." This represents Mount Meru. Imagine that you are building a complete universe, with seven golden mountains surrounding Mount Meru, seven lakes, and so on.

The side facing you, at your wrist, is east. Starting from this eastern direction, build the existing world by making offerings at the eastern, northern, western, and southern directions of the mandala. As you are doing this, recite:

Ah Yam Ram Mam Kham Shag Sa Le Sang Nge So Ha

The four worlds of Mount Meru are as follows.

The color of the eastern world is white and its shape is a half moon. The precious symbol of that world is a vase full of treasures (rinpoche bumpa).

The color of the northern world is green and its shape is a square. The precious symbol of that world is a tree giving fruit that provides all with perfect nourishment (paksam shing).

The color of the western world is red and its shape is a circle. The precious symbol of that world is the cow that provides endless milk that fulfills every wish (dö jö ba).

The southern world is the world in which we live. The color of the southern world is blue and its shape is that of a human shoulder blade. The precious symbol of that world is a jewel (norbu rinpoche).

These are the four colors, four shapes, and four symbols allocated to the worlds of the four directions around Mount Meru.

The next step in offering the mandala is building the eight continents around the world. Each direction is linked to two continents, which are located to its right and left. Recite:

Ah Yam Ram Mam Kham Shag Sa Le Sang Nge So Ha

To the right and left of the east are Koring and Kotung, to the right and left of the north are Gyagti and Gyogti, to the right and left of the west are Marzhi and Tengzhi, and to the right and left of the south are Khalon and Telgyum. Next, recite:

Chöd Phur Sa Le Ha Lo Seng

Add the offerings to the eight continents and the four directions as follows: in the east, the golden sun; in the north, the seven jewels; in the west, the white moon; and in the south, the eight auspicious symbols. Then put additional offerings on the mandala. Build the mandala gradually by adding three rings so as to allow for more offerings and complete the mandala.

In this universe you have manifested, imagine offering the most beautiful forms, the most pleasant sounds and smells, the most delicious tastes, the softest textures, the most beautiful ornaments, and limitless precious objects of the god and human realms, whatever is existing, such as a mountain of jewels, auspicious diamonds, a forest of medicines, fields of well-grown crops, and even your own life and fortune, your bliss and pleasure, your retinues and company, your virtuous deeds, and those of all sentient beings, and all the virtuous deeds of the three times. All are offered to the supreme objects of refuge. Ask that they please accept these offerings happily and with great bliss. In return, ask that they bless you and protect you from the internal and external defilements, and bless you to achieve self-realization at this session of practice. Visualize that you make these offerings to the enlightened ones, and repeat the mandala offering. When your hands become tired, place the mandala on an altar or table you have arranged.

Then recite this prayer of the mandala offering:

Eh Ma, jung ngai teng du ri rab ri dün dang
Ling zhi ling tren chi nang dhö yön che
Nyi dhe gyen pa je wa trag gya dhi
Dhag gi lö lang bul lo zhe su söl

On the foundation of the five elements, Mount Meru and the seven
golden mountains,
Including the external and internal precious objects of the four worlds
and eight continents,
Millions of universes, decorated with suns and moons,
Please accept and bless this offering from the core of my heart.

While you recite the prayer, do the mandala offering gesture (chag gya). After each prayer, take a small amount of the offering material from your lap or from the table and offer it to the mandala. Use the mandala objects at least one hundred times, but no more than three hundred times. After this, change the materials on the mandala.

When you change the materials, recite the following prayer:

La ma der sheg yi dam lha tsok la
Dro wa kun dang che te kyab su chi
Nya ngen mi dha zhug par söl wa dhep
Thug je tang dral med par zhug du söl

In the assembly of lama, yidam, and enlightened ones
I and all sentient beings take refuge with great joy.
Please remain forever to bless us in this suffering world.
Protect us without decreasing your blessings and compassion.

Wish for the everlasting blessings and protection of the four supreme objects of refuge. Then slowly remove the offering materials, beginning with the eastern direction and ending with the southern direction, and while doing so, recite the following prayer:

Bön nyid sem nyid ye ne mi gyur te
Tsig dang sem chen dhü je mi tag pa
Leg je de la nye je gang lag pa
La ma der shek nam la zöd par söl
Ten du kyod par ma lag te
Lar yang dro we dön la thug je gong
Om Ah Da Da De De Chöd Chöd Sa Le Ha Lo Seng

The nature of Bön and mind is nondistraction from the very beginning.

Words, all sentient beings, and all compounded things are impermanent.
Whatever faults were ever in the actions,
I confess to the lama and the enlightened ones.
I realize you will not be here forever,
But please care for and protect all sentient beings with your compassion.
Om Ah Da Da De De Chöd Chöd Sa Le Ha Lo Seng

Contemplation

At the conclusion of the practice, all sentient beings are transformed into the four objects of refuge, and all are dissolved into Shen Lha Ökar. The lama is dissolved into light, and then into oneself. Finally, oneself and everything in the existing world are transformed into the state of emptiness. Remain there for as long as you are able.

Dedication

After performing the mandala offering practice and meditation, dedicate the merit you have cultivated by this practice to all sentient beings by reciting the dedication prayer as given on page 83 for the first preliminary practice. Complete a total of 100,000 mandala offerings.

PRELIMINARY PRACTICE 5:
CONNECTING WITH THE TEACHER

The essential aspect of the preliminary practice of connecting with the teacher (lamai naljor) is to open your inner wisdom. It is very important to receive blessings from your teacher to support you. Whatever teachings you may receive, even the shortest recitation prayers or oral transmissions, will depend on your teacher; all the teachings have to be transmitted from the teacher. No one in the past has ever achieved enlightenment without following the instructions of a teacher.

Therefore, it is even more important for us ordinary people to follow and respect the teachers. From the very first moment of your practice until you accomplish your goal, you must follow your teacher and practice to view the teacher as a manifestation of the enlightened ones in the form of a human body. Especially when you follow the deeper levels of the teachings such as Sang Ngag and Dzogchen, in order to receive accomplishments — both temporary and ultimate qualities — you are relying on the teacher's blessings and powers.

According to your view and respect for the teacher, you will receive the teacher's blessings. By viewing your teacher as the real presence of the Buddha or the enlightened ones, you will receive blessings, powers, and teachings like nectar. If you view him as a businessman, his blessings and teachings will affect you more like an object for sale. And if you view him as an ordinary person, accordingly, all his blessings may just be like food.

It is not the teacher's expectations that will make a difference for his students with regard to his blessings and teachings. From his point of view, it is the same whether the students respect him or not. How much blessing they will receive depends on the individual students themselves.

Therefore, always try to follow the teacher tirelessly, fulfill his instructions, and do everything possible not to disappoint his wisdom mind, which may obstruct the development of your inner practice.

One of the famous teachers of Bön known as Dulwa Rinpoche

said, "Without hesitation and without separating from the visualization of the lama over your crown wheel (chiwo dechen gyi khorlo) even for a moment, pray and seek blessings from him." It is a simple method for achieving all the qualities of the enlightened ones and receiving their blessings so as to achieve realization of the true state of mind. Once you have achieved this realization of your true nature of mind, it is like a butter lamp which lights up the dark.

You have to practice this teaching with a completely pure and genuine inner intention, genuinely giving rise to thoughts of trust and inspiration with respect to your teacher's qualities. Practice in this way until you actualize the inner experience.

How to Meditate on Connecting with the Teacher

Meditation Posture

While doing the practice of lamai naljor, sit in the proper meditation posture (see full description in the beginning of "How to Meditate on Generating the Mind of Enlightenment" on pages 78–79).

Visualizations and Recitations

The practice of connecting with the teacher, lamai naljor, develops the student's inner wisdom. Imagine that one foot above your crown wheel is a jeweled throne supported by eight lions. On that jeweled throne is another throne in the form of a lotus with sun and moon cushions. On the cushions sits your root lama, who is the combination of the qualities of compassion, wisdom, and love of all the enlightened beings in the three times of past, present, and future. Your root lama is in the form of the Enlightened One of Compassion, Shen Lha Ökar.

His perfect form is facing you. All the experiential lineage holders extend from above his crown to Kuntu Zangpo, the Primordial Enlightened One, as outlined in the visualization for the practice of generating the mind of enlightenment on pages 79–80.

Visualize the objects of refuge as described above very clearly, feeling their presence and focusing on them single-pointedly, without being disturbed by any other thoughts. Consider that from today on you will lead yourself and all sentient beings on the pathway until all achieve enlightenment.

You should think, "Apart from you, teacher, and the objects of refuge, we have no one to rely on. Please purify and remove all obstacles, even the smallest karmic trace, from all sentient beings and myself, and protect us from all obstacles — internal, external, and secret — and bless us to complete the pathway of practice, which is our desire." Then, seriously aspire from your heart, "During this session and on this cushion, may I be blessed with the wisdom of self-realization, by clearing away all obstacles and distractions to the absolute mind of enlightenment."

The sign of success in this practice occurs when, without any doubt or hesitation and with complete devotion, tears run from your eyes and the hair of your body stands on end. This is the sign of devotion arising from within with full trust and belief. Then, recite the lamai naljor prayer:

Eh Ma Ho
Chi tsug dhe wa chen pö pho dang dhu
Din chen tsa we la ma la söl wa dhep

Sang gye sem su tön pa rin po che
Rang ngo rang gi she par jin gyi lob
In the palace of great bliss on my crown
I pray to the kind root lama,
The jewel who shows me the enlightened one in my mind.
Bless me to recognize my own nature.

Then, from the core of your mind, think of your own teacher and mentally say to him, "You are the one whom I depend on and trust, so please bless me to overcome this suffering and realize my own nature of mind."

Following this prayer, nectar of wisdom will flow from the heart of Kuntu Zangpo, and flow through the lineage holders to the crown of Shen Lha Ökar. Then it flows out of Shen Lha Ökar's heart, and flows to the crown of all sentient beings, including yourself. Visualize this image clearly because it will purify your inner and outer impurities, and all sentient beings will be transformed into pure bodies of light. Then gradually the deities and protectors and enlightened ones you have visualized are transformed into light, and dissolve into the lama, who is the root of the Three Jewels. He is inseparable from the three bodies of the enlightened ones. He is also the combined nature of hundreds of mandalas (kyilkhor yongkyi ngadag).

Imagine the lama sitting above you as a great liberator of all sentient beings and pray "Lama Rinpoche, Lama Rinpoche, Lama Rinpoche" and supplicate him from your heart with this prayer:

Dag gi lho ghe war gyur war zed du söl
Ghe wa lam la dro war zed du söl

Lam thar chin par zed du söl
Khye par dha ta dhug sa dhi ru nyam tog khye par chen gyud la
kye war zed du söl

Please transform my conceptual mind into virtuous deeds,
Please transform all my virtuous deeds into the pathway of
enlightenment,
Bless me to accomplish the pathway of practice,
Bless me to develop extraordinary experience and realization on
this cushion.

This prayer is for your daily practice. If you are fulfilling the required accumulations of the preliminary practices, recite the lamai naljor prayers as given above 100,000 times.

Before you conclude the session, pray to receive the blessings of the four empowerments (wang zhi) from your teacher:

Lama Rinpoche, Lama Rinpoche, Lama Rinpoche,
Dag gi lü la ku yi wang chok kur tu söl

Lama Rinpoche, Lama Rinpoche, Lama Rinpoche,
Please give me the empowerment of perfect body.

Visualize that from the lama's forehead a white AH syllable, made of light, enters into your forehead. With this blessing, the three nonvirtuous deeds of the body, taking life, stealing, and sexual misconduct, are purified. This will also purify negative energy and prevent it from increasing within your body. Imagine that you have received the empowerment of the lama's pure body and that your body is transformed into the perfect body of the enlightened ones. Then say:

Lama Rinpoche, Lama Rinpoche, Lama Rinpoche,
Dag gi ngag la sung gi wang chok kur tu söl

Lama Rinpoche, Lama Rinpoche, Lama Rinpoche,
Please give me the empowerment of perfect speech.

Visualize a red OM syllable, made of light, coming from the lama's throat and entering into your throat. In this way, the four nonvirtuous deeds of speech, telling lies, divisive talk, harsh language, and idle gossip, are purified. This also purifies the negative energy of the winds that allows negative speech to increase. From that, you receive the speech blessings of the lama, and imagine that you have received the empowerment to transform your speech into the manifestation body of the enlightened ones. Then recite:

Lama Rinpoche, Lama Rinpoche, Lama Rinpoche,
Dag gi yid la thug kyi wang chok kur tu söl

Lama Rinpoche, Lama Rinpoche, Lama Rinpoche,
Please give me the empowerment of perfect wisdom mind.

Visualize that, from the heart of the lama, a dark blue HUNG syllable, made of light, is transformed into your heart. It purifies the three nonvirtuous deeds of your mind, which are wishing others ill, creating the attitude that damages others, and having wrong views. This purifies the negative energies of the "spot of light" (thigle) that represent negative thoughts developing in your mind. In this way, you receive the blessings of the lama, and the empowerment to transform your mind into the mind of the primordial state. Then recite:

Lama Rinpoche, Lama Rinpoche, Lama Rinpoche,
Dag la khyed par ye she kyi wang chok kur tu söl

Lama Rinpoche, Lama Rinpoche, Lama Rinpoche,
Please empower me with your enlightened wisdom.

Visualize the lama and the throne descending from space and arriving at your crown wheel. Imagine that the size of the lama's body is reduced to the size of the span from your thumb to your index finger. See his body as clear and perfect, with all the details, with a smiling face and sparkling eyes. Focus on his happy and joyful mind for a while.

Then reduce your visualization of the lama to the size of your thumb joint (one inch or so) and imagine that the lama is now at the level of your throat wheel. As before, continue to see the lama's body as clear and perfect in all its details with his smiling face and so on. Focus on the joyful state of the lama.

Then the lama's body is reduced from one inch to the size of a grain of barley and he moves to the eight-petaled lotus at your heart wheel. His perfect body is still clear, shining, and bright, his expression is happy, and his eyes are sparkling. Focus on the joyful state of the lama's mind for some time and then, still focused in this way, visualize the lama's body becoming smaller and smaller, until your mind and the lama's mind dissolve into each other. In this way, you completely purify all the negative actions and defilements accumulated within yourself in the base of all (kunzhi). Imagine that you have received the empowerment of the ultimate state.

Contemplation

Imagine that you have transformed the lama's self-arising wisdom into yourself and received the empowerment of the ultimate state. In that state, without modifying or following past, present, or future thoughts, remain in stillness like a cloudless sky or a very peaceful ocean before it is disturbed by the wind. Relax in this natural state in order to "watch the inner state of the lama's face." This means remain in the true natural state of your mind, inseparable from the true quality of the lama's mind.

Dedication

When you emerge from this state, by reciting the dedication prayers on page 83, you dedicate the root of all your virtuous deeds to the liberation of all sentient beings, as the great spiritual warriors and enlightened ones of the past have dedicated.

PRELIMINARY PRACTICE 6: PROSTRATIONS

Prostrations mainly involve movement of the physical body. The main purpose of prostrations is to purify the nonvirtuous deeds and negativities of the body. In Tibetan, the word chak means sweeping away the impurities of the body. One does prostrations in front of a statue, in a temple, in a holy pace, in front of one's teacher, and so on.

If the right material object is lacking, one can prostrate anywhere by visualizing the four supreme refuge objects above oneself.

In this practice there are two kind of prostrations: the full prostrations (kyang chak), where you lay down the full length of your body; and the easier and shorter prostrations (kum chak), where the five branches of your body (your forehead, both hands, and both knees) touch the ground while you do a recitation prayer with the visualization of the deities and the enlightened ones.

The most important aspect of this practice is again one's pure intention. In Tibet there is a tradition of circumambulating holy mountains like Kongpo Bön Ri, the mountain of Bön in the Kongpo Valley blessed by Tönpa Shenrab himself, by doing prostrations after every step.

Prostrations are not the only way to purify bodily negativities. You can also purify them by circumambulating temples or other holy mountains. Another way is also to participate in the construction of a temple or other holy place such as a stupa or a sand mandala.

How to Do Prostrations

Short Prostrations

Stand straight and bring your arms up in front of you, palms up. This symbolizes offering the whole world. Lift your hands higher and when you reach the level of your crown wheel, put your palms together. This is the offering to the enlightened ones. Touch your hands to your crown wheel, then to your throat wheel, and then to your heart wheel. In this way, you receive the blessings of the body, speech, and mind of the enlightened ones. Next, sweep your hands down your body, symbolizing sweeping away the negativities and kneel down and touch the ground with the palms of your hands in front of your knees. Then bend down and touch the floor in front of your body with your forehead. All five branches of your body — both knees, both palms of your hands, and your forehead — should touch the ground properly at the same time. Remain in this position for a few seconds, stand up, and repeat these same steps three times. After the third time, stand up and repeat only the part with the hands. Doing prostrations (chak) purifies your negativities of body, mind, and speech.

Full Prostrations

Stand straight and bring your arms up in front of you, palms up. This symbolizes offering to the whole world. Lift your hands higher, and when you reach the level of your crown wheel put your palms together. This is the offering to the enlightened ones. Touch your hands to your crown wheel, then your throat wheel, and then your heart wheel. This way you receive the blessings of the body, speech, and mind of the enlightened ones. Then sweep your hands down your body, symbolizing sweeping away the negativities. Kneel down and stretch your body flat on the ground, bring your arms and hands straight over your head, flat on the floor. Remain in this position for a few seconds, then stand up and repeat these same steps three times. After the third, stand up and repeat only the part with the hands.

The text says that the more you challenge yourself and the more pure intention you have for this practice, the more blessings you will receive. Thus, the most important thing is to have proper motivation, full devotion, and precise visualization. Otherwise, doing prostrations will be just physical exercise. It is best to do prostrations in holy places. It is believed that you multiply merits by cultivating this practice.

Recitations

While doing your prostrations, recite the prayers for the practice of taking refuge as given on pages 89–90. In addition, you can recite the three essential recitations (see "Preliminary Practices 7–9" below) with each prostration. This allows completion of all five of these practices at one time.

Dedication

By completing 100,000 prostrations, you will purify all the nonvirtuous deeds of the body. As with all the preliminary practices, at the end of each practice session, recite the dedication prayer as given on page 83 for the first preliminary practice.

PRELIMINARY PRACTICES 7–9:
THE THREE ESSENTIAL RECITATIONS

The Three Essential Recitations (Nyingpo Namsum) are the Recitation of the Enlightened One of Compassion (Sa Le Öd), the Recitation of Dhe Chog Rinchin Dolma (Ma Tri), and the Recitation of Ngensong Dong Tuk (Dhu Tri Su). Each of the Nyingpo Namsum are outlined below.

Sa Le Öd: The Recitation of the Enlightened One of Compassion

Ah Om Hung A Ah Kar Sa Le Öd Ah Yang Om Dhu

	Symbolic Meaning
Ah	Primordial State of Kuntu Zangpo (Bön Ku)
Om	Perfected Body (Zog Ku)
Hung	Manifestation or Emanation Body (Tul Ku)
A	Enlightened One of Compassion (Shen Lha Ökar)
Ah Kar	Pure Nature of Bön (Bön Ku)
Sa Le Öd	Clear Light (Sal Cha)
Ah Yang	Unborn Wisdom (Kye Med)
Om	Five Bodies and Five Wisdoms (Ku Nga Yeshe Nga)
Dhu	Remain As It Is, in Its Own Nature (Ne Lug)

Ma Tri: The Recitation of Dhechok Rinchin Dolma

Om Ma Tri Mu Ye Sa Le Dhu

	Symbolic Meaning
Om	White; Tönpa Shenrab, who represents compassion.
Ma	Red; Sherab Chamma, who represents wisdom.
Tri	Purple; Mucho Dem Dug, who transforms anger and hate by means of love, thus purifying the hell realms.
Mu	Red; Sangwa Ngang Ring, who transforms greed and desire by means of generosity, thus purifying the realms of the hungry ghosts.
Ye	Blue; Tisang Rangzhi, who transforms ignorance and confusion by means of knowledge and wisdom, thus purifying the animal realm.
Sa	Yellow; Drajin Pungpa, who transforms envy and jealousy by means of openness and flexibility, thus purifying the human realm.
Le	Grey; Chegyal Parti, who transforms pride and arrogance by means of peacefulness, thus purifying the realm of the demi-gods.
Dhu	White; Yeshen Tsugphud, who transforms laziness and sloth by means of diligence and vigor, thus purifying the god realm.

Among these eight seed syllables, the first two sequentially represent Tönpa Shenrab and Sherab Chamma, the loving mother, and the next six are the seed syllables of the Enlightened Ones of the Six Realms (Dhulwa Shendrug), each of them being an emanation of Tönpa Shenrab, whose purpose is to liberate all sentient beings.

Dhu Tri Su: The Recitation of Ngensong Dong Tuk

Before doing this recitation, recite the following prayer:

*Khor we sem chen tham ched thuk che thar pa den pi pal
Shenrab Tönpi ku la chak tsal lo.
A Kar Ah Me Dhu Tri Su Nag Po Zhi Zhi Mal Mal So Ha*

*I offer prostrations to Tönpa Shenrab, the great being
Who liberates all sentient beings by means of compassion.
A Kar Ah Me Dhu Tri Su Nag Po Zhi Zhi Mal Mal So Ha*

	Symbolic Meaning
A Kar	Pure state of mind
Ah Me	Clear aspect of wisdom
Dhu Tri Su	Purifying the suffering of the three lower realms
Nag Po	Eliminating negative karmas
Zhi Zhi	Pacifying the suffering of this cyclic world
Mal Mal	Bringing joy and happiness
So Ha	Removing all misunderstanding and discriminatory thinking

Once you have finished this recitation, recite the following prayer of profound praise (zab töd):

A Kar sem nyid nam par dak
Ah Me ye she öd du sal
Du Ti Su yi ngen song jong
Nag Po le kyi dhig drib dak
Zhi Zhi khor we dug ngal zhi
Mal Mal dhe we sem dang dhen
So Ha lok tok ru ta jom

Dug ngal zhi jed nying po dhi
Khor we ngen song dong tuk ne
Dro nam Bön nyid ying su sang gye shok

A Kar, the pure state of mind,
Ah Me, the clarity and radiance of wisdom,
Du Ti purifies the suffering of the three lower realms,
Nag Po eliminates nonvirtuous deeds and obscurations,
Zhi Zhi pacifies the suffering of this cyclic world,
Mal Mal brings joy and happiness,
So Ha subdues misconceptions and discriminatory thoughts.

This is the essential recitation to pacify suffering.
By stirring the depths of the suffering of this cyclic world
May all sentient beings be liberated!

After you have completed the practice of the three essential recitations, perform the dedication prayer on page 83 as you have with all the preliminary practices.

The Ngöndro practices presented here provide beginning practitioners with the necessary foundation that opens the door to the vast world of the Bön teachings. After gaining an understanding of compassion for all sentient beings as the heart of the practice, many students then ask their teacher to describe the philosophical basis of the teachings and give further instructions for deepening their own experience. These next steps occur through the actual practices (ngo zhi), which include the Phowa and Bardo instructions, as well as the introduction to the Natural State of Mind (Sem Trid). Once we have trained thoroughly with a well-qualified teacher in all these practices with pure motivation and compassion for all sentient beings, we are well along the pathway to enlightenment.

Glossary

Bön A Shamanic tradition under the name of "Bön" existed in Tibet long before Yungdrung Bön (eternal Bön), the teachings of Tönpa Shenrab.

Bön Nyid Nature of Bön or nature of all existence, both absolute and relative.

Bönpo A Bön practitioner.

Bön Shen A Bön master. A term unique to Bön, "Shen" is from Zhang Zhung, and has several meanings. Bön Shen gave spiritual guidance to the early kings of Tibet. Sometimes Bön Shen can refer to an ordinary practitioner of Bön, but here it refers to those masters who have achieved high realization (Bön Shen Rigzin).

Chamma Loving Mother. She is the chief female deity in Bön and also the mother (yum) of all the enlightened ones of the three times (past, present, and future). She is also known as Yum Chen Sherab Chamma, the great loving mother of wisdom. Her twenty-one manifestations are known as Chamma Nyer Chig.

Changbu A changbu is an offering object made of tsampa (roasted barley flour). Prints of the five fingers are imprinted on it to represent our five senses: sense of body (zug), sense of hearing (da), sense of smell (di), sense of taste (ro), and sense of feeling (reg ja). It is offered to the evil spirits causing sickness to tame and satisfy them.

Chok Chu Dewar Shekpa or **Chok Chu Sangye** The Enlightened Ones of the Ten Directions. The four cardinal points and the four intermediate cardinal points together with up and down form the ten directions. Every one of these ten directions is filled with numerous enlightened ones.

Circumambulate. See Kor Ra.

Dho Generally, Dho refers to text. Here it includes the philosophical teachings of Bön. The Dho school, mainly taught by Tönpa Shenrab in his third turning of the wheel of Bön, is divided into outer (dho), inner (nag), and secret (Dzogchen) teachings.

Dol Lam Dzogpa Chenpo Pathway of Self-Liberation. According to Dzogchen, the five poisons and impure visions are overcome, without applying the methods of renunciation or transformation, by leaving things in their true state of "nature as it is." This means to apply a method where all things are allowed to self-liberate.

Dzogchen Great Perfection. The highest or ninth level of Bön.

Gang Ti Se Mount Kailash. A very sacred mountain to the Bönpos, connected to Zhang Zhung Meri, a deity who still resides there. Its name, Gang Ti Se, originated from the Zhang Zhung language: "Ti" means mountain of ice and "Se" means god or deity.

Gom Lam Path of Meditation. Highest and fourth stage in the pathway of training.

Gong Ter Mind Treasure. Spontaneously arisen meditational experiences of great masters given as teachings in poetry or prose.

Gyur Lam Ngag Pathway of Transformation. Following the pathway of transformation means to practice according to the Tantric view, to realize the whole universe in its true nature and pure dimension of existence (dag zhing), to transform all sentient beings from their ordinary level into their true form as deities, and to transform the five poisons into the five wisdoms.

Jor Lam Path of Preparation. Second of the four training pathways to enlightenment.

Karma Action. In a more general context, karma refers to the law of cause and result.

Khadro Sky Walker. Female manifestations of the enlightened ones, who protect practitioners in this cyclic existence. In the Tantric view, khadros are the source of accomplishment (ngodup) and also one of the inner refuge fields.

Kongpo Bön Ri In the Kongpo valley during Tönpa Shenrab's visit to Tibet, after subduing the local evil spirits and the demon Khyabpa, and giving the basic teachings of Bön, he blessed the mountain (Muri Mukpo Tse) as a holy pilgrimage site. Since then, it has been known as Kongpo Bön Ri, the Bön Mountain of Kongpo. To this day, it is visited year round by Bönpo pilgrims from all over Tibet.

Kor Ra Circumambulate. To circle a holy object or temple by walking or doing prostrations around it. This is a traditional practice for accumulating good merit and purifying karmic negativities. Practitioners circumambulate temples, stupas, or holy mountains.

Kuntu Zangpo All-Good. Generally, this means the pure state of the Primordial Enlightened One, but it also refers to the holy, central part of the mountain Kongpo Bön Ri where there is a very special rock into which Tönpa Shenrab transferred the energy and blessings of his wisdom mind, and hid several holy objects. Since then, it has been known as the heart of Kuntu Zangpo.

Lam Ma Zhugpa Nonpath. A person is referred to as being on a nonpath when he or she is not practicing and will thus never achieve self-realization.

Lama Highest Mother. A spiritual teacher of the highest importance to a practitioner.

Lamai Naljor Practice of connecting with the teacher.

Lop Lam Path of Training. There are four training paths: tsog lam, jor lam, thong lam, and gom lam. Highly realized practitioners who have achieved the mind of enlightenment and realized the nature of mind are on the path of training, or lop lam.

Lued or **Tue Lued** In general there are many forms of lued, which are offering objects made of tsampa. There is a special form of lued called tue lued, which is a representation of one's own body. Through the blessing water applied on the tue lued one washes away sicknesses, negativities, and bad karmas from the past and offers them with dedication prayers to the lower spirits.

Lung Oral transmission. The reading of a teaching text out loud by a lama to his disciples, thus connecting the disciples to the lineage.

Mi Lop Lam Beyond the training path, the resultant state of enlightenment.

Naza Gö Drug The six robes worn by monks. These special monks' robes are: the lotus crown (padzhu), the yellow upper robe (medgö) worn only at special ceremonies but carried at all times, the upper red robe (meyog) worn all the time (also known as zen), the upper shirt (tögag) that for Bönpo monks is mostly blue, the lower robe (mäsham) in maroon colors (also known as shamthap), and the shoes (pälham) mainly made of grass or wool. These are the robes that monks can wear, which originated when Tönpa Shenrab renounced his princely life.

Olmo Lung Ring An enlightened realm, the birthplace of Tönpa Shenrab, and the original source of Bön (see Chapter 1).

Om In the Bön tradition, the syllable Om represents the five perfect bodies and the wisdom of the enlightened ones. These five bodies are: the primordial state of the wisdom body (Bön ku), the perfected body (zog ku), the manifestation body (tul ku), the body that is pure by its nature (ngowo nyi ku), and the absolute perfected body free from spontaneously arising obscurations (ngon par jangchup pi ku).

Parchin Chu Ten transcendental practices: (1) generosity (jinpa), (2) morality (tsultrim), (3) patience (zödpa), (4) enthusiasm (tsondu), (5) concentration (samten), (6) contemplation (top), (7) compassion (nyingje), (8) dedication (monlam), (9) method and means (thab), (10) wisdom (sherab).

Pong Lam Dho The Pathway of Renunciation. Following the pathway of renunciation according to the middle path school, the highest level in the Dho tradition.

Rinchen Ze Nga Five Precious Objects. These are the five objects every monk must possess: a shaving blade (pudri), sewing needles (khap), a vase for blessing waters (trubum), a staff topped with a stupa (kharsil or höru) that may be used as an object to be circumambulated during prayers, and a begging bowl (zhikur or lhungze) used to ask for food.

Rinpoche Precious One. An honorary title commonly used when addressing an incarnate lama.

Sangye The enlightened one(s). One who is completely purified of defilements and who has achieved all the qualities of perfection, such as omniscient wisdom and compassion; fully enlightened.

Semchen Thamched All sentient beings. Those beings who are not yet free from ignorance and who are suffering from the results of their own misdeeds in this cyclic world.

Terma Rediscovered treasure. A terma is any object such as a statue or a text discovered by great masters from hidden treasures.

Tertön Treasure revealer or rediscovery master; one who finds or rediscovers holy objects that were hidden in the past, often during times when Bönpos were being persecuted. Tertöns are usually reincarnations or manifestations of early masters who hid the treasures.

Thong Lam Path of Seeing. The third stage of the training pathway to enlightenment.

Tönpa Shenrab. Founder and enlightened teacher of Bön.

Torma; Red Torma Offering cakes. A torma is an offering object made of tsampa. Tormas are often painted red to symbolize blood. Some evil spirits and local deities can be tamed only by blood offerings. Since the time of Tönpa Shenrab's visit to Tibet, the blood offerings have been replaced by red tormas so that no animals are sacrificed.

Trid Teaching or instruction. The method, following wang and lung, of giving clear and detailed instructions to disciples according to the transmissions of unbroken lineage teachings.

Tsang Tsukpa Ordained monk. One who has renounced worldly life by taking vows, entering monastic life, and strictly engaging in practice and studies.

Tsog Lam Path of Accumulation. The first pathway of the four training paths to enlightenment.

Tul Ku Manifestation body of an enlightened one.

Wang Empowerment. A ritual ceremony in which a lama empowers his disciples to do the practices of a specific esoteric tradition by connecting them with his lineage; introducing disciples to their own self-nature.

Yeshe Nga The Five Wisdoms.

> *Wisdom of Emptiness* (Tongnyid Yeshe) is the empty aspect of the mind;
>
> *Mirrorlike Wisdom* (Melong Yeshe) is the clear aspect of awareness (Rigpa) by which the nature of mind is realized;
>
> *Wisdom of Equality* (Nyamnyid Yeshe) is the unification of awareness (Rigpa) and the empty aspect of the nature of mind;
>
> *Wisdom of Discrimination* (Sortog Yeshe) is the clear realization of the distinction between the clear aspect of awareness (Rigpa) and the empty nature of mind within;
>
> *Wisdom of Accomplishment* (Jadrub Yeshe) is the spontaneously arising perfect action of wisdom and compassion within the state of its nature.

Yulchok Ne Zhi Four Supreme Objects. In general, objects referred to as supreme are holy objects. In this case, the Four Supreme Objects are also called the Four Jewels. They are: (1) Sangye, the enlightened one(s); (2) Bön, the teachings; (3) Yungdrung Sempa, those who have achieved the mind of enlightenment; (4) the lama or root teacher.

Yungdrung A term designating the Bön religion. As a symbol, its meaning is unique to Bön: "yung" is the unborn, absolute truth, free of any inherent nature, and "drung" is constantly arising; therefore, Bön is the unification of the two truths: absolute truth and relative truth.

Yungdrung Bön Eternal Bön. The teachings of Tönpa Shenrab; the native religion of Tibet.

Yungdrung Chag Shing Unique symbol of Bön. A holy object, it is held by Tönpa Shenrab in his right hand and symbolizes the turning of the wheel of Bön. The yungdrung chag shing has two yungdrungs, one at each end.

Yungdrung Sempa Yungdrung-minded ones. Those who have achieved the heart and mind of the enlightened ones and who have attained at least the first stage of the path, tsok lam, or the path of accumulation. Those whose practices are done in order to achieve enlightenment for the benefit of all sentient beings.

Zhang Zhung Source of Bön in Tibet. The kingdom of Zhang Zhung existed until the end of the eighth century when it was integrated into Tibet after the death of Ligmincha, its last king. In early times, the kingdom of Zhang Zhung was the closest neighboring land to Tibet, extending from what is known today as the upper part of northwestern Tibet, through parts of Nepal and Northern India (Kashmir, Ladakh, Zanskar, Kinnaur, Spiti, etc.) to Pakistan (Kashmir) and China (the Karakoram area). Mount Kailash was the center of Zhang Zhung. Most of the Bön teachings have been translated from the Zhang Zhung language into Tibetan.